INDIAN PHILOSOPHY
Arguments and Counterarguments

K. SRINIVAS

GYAN

First Published, 2018

Published by
Gyan Publishing House
5, Ansari Road
Daryaganj, New Delhi-110002
Phone: 9811692060
E-mail: books@gyanbooks.com
Printed at: G. Print Process, Delhi.

Cataloging in Publication Data--DK
Courtesy: D.K. Agencies (P) Ltd. <docinfo@dkagencies.com>

Srinivas, K. (Kunchapudi), 1955- author.
Indian philosophy : arguments and counterarguments / K. Srinivas.
pages cm
Includes bibliographical references and index.
ISBN 9788121214506

1. Philosophy, Indic. I. Title.

B131.S65 2018 DDC 181.4 23

To

Sriman N.C. Lakshmanacharyulu

Dr. K. Sunil Kumar

Contents

Foreword

Indian philosophy is unique and distinctive in several ways. First and foremost it is the oldest ancient philosophy of the world as roots and seeds of both the orthodox and heterodox schools of Indian philosophy can be traced to the Vedas, including *Ṛksamhita* which is the earliest available book of the humanity. Speculations regarding the fundamentals of philosophy are clearly spoken in the hymns such as *Nāsadiyasūkta, Puruṣasūkta* and hymns dedicated to various forms of natural gods. *Upaniṣads*, of course, are well acknowledged sources of Indian Philosophy which, though chronologically later than the *Samhitas*, are earlier than well-known philosophical schools, such as Greeks.

Indian philosophy is school-based and not thinker-based as most of other philosophies are. As every school of philosophy has a long history of development running into millions of years, understanding various theories and doctrines needs greater effort and endurance.

The development of Indian philosophy is in the mode/form of inter-school rivalry and/or interaction. This causes difficulty in identifying component of philosophical development distinctively different from dialectical discussions.

It is worth mentioning that the development of Indian philosophy is based on commentarial tradition than on individual texts or treatises. In fact, the number of original texts in Indian philosophy is far less than the number of commentaries on various texts. This causes ambiguity while identifying the author-wise individual thought.

Another challenging problem is that the source languages in which both the orthodox and heterodox schools of Indian philosophical texts and commentaries are written i.e. Sanskrit, Pāli and Prākrit, have ceased to exist in common popular usage centuries ago. This poses hardship to decipher the exact meaning of technical terms.

It is noteworthy to observe that philosophy is of the nature of speculative contemplation and reasoning. Indian Philosophy is, however, interpretative too in addition to this. Because, we accept verbal testimony also as one of the valid means of knowledge and with regard to a number of systems of Indian philosophy, the Vedic and the *Upaniṣadic* statements carry supreme authority to the extent that the reasoning should be made in tune with them and not contradicting them. This situation compelled Indian philosophers to resort to interpreting the Vedic, *Upaniṣadic* and *Purāṇik* passages in such a way as to suit to their philosophical position. This situation led to the origination of Science of Textual Interpretation, Mīmāṁsā and *Shābdabodha*, unique systems / branches of Indian philosophy.

As Sanskrit is an etymological language, each term carries various shades of innate meanings, derived on the basis of its etymology and such shades of meanings do have a bearing on the concept expressed by the term. On account of this, it is very difficult to find one to one word in other languages. This creates greater challenge in translating and understanding the concepts through translations. For example, if we try to translate *ātman* it signifies distinctive meaning and both the possible terms in English, such as soul and self, are inadequate to express the meaning in full.

It is sad to observe that the history of Indian philosophy is, to a large extent, shrouded in darkness. Except in systems like Jainism, Buddhism and in respect of a few authors in other systems, authentic dates are not known for majority of authors. History of Indian philosophy is mostly reconstructed on the strength of commentarial tradition and other internal evidences. This becomes an impediment in tracing the historical development of thought.

Lastly, in the case of majority of Indian systems of philosophy the origination is traced to concerned *sūtras*. In none of the systems of philosophy elsewhere such origination is seen. This situation raises a very important question regarding the history of origination of Indian philosophy for a sutra or *kārikā* can, at best, be in the form of conclusion of thought, speculation, reasoning or discussion, but, certainly, not be the beginning of the thought, speculation, reasoning or discussion. This fact can be vouched even with regard to modern sciences and philosophy where after centuries of research a conclusion in the form of an equation or law or principle emerged, such as '$E=mc^2$'. Therefore, a system of thought cannot be originated with a sutra. Mention of several names of *ācāryas* in the *sūtras* also tends to support this. Therefore, the origin of Indian philosophy must be much older than what it has been taken to be.

All these distinctions make us realize that there are several factors which cause different kinds of challenges while pursuing Indian philosophical studies. Therefore, there is a need for such books which can illumine the pathway to reach the goals in Indian Philosophy.

Professor Srinivas deserves rich compliments for making such an effort to help the scholars and students of Indian philosophy to obtain required clarity in the areas supposed to be dark such as *apohavāda,* issue of inter-relation between the philosophies of Gauḍapāda and Buddhists, concepts of *aprathaksiddhi* and *dharmabhūtajňāna* of Śrī Rāmānuja, problem of space and time in less analyzed system of Pūrva-Mīmāṁsā and so on. Such a systematic, comprehensive view of Indian philosophical system, clearly defining its nature and scope adopting proper periodization and relating writers and Schools firmly to changing philosophical conditions had not been attempted. Written in an accessible style, this book can be an essential reference to anyone interested in Indian philosophy.

I appreciate the effort of Professor Srinivas in exhibiting his control while dealing with such difficult topics as they are flooded with dialectical cross currents in the source books. In dealing with such baffling schools of thought, teaching and research experience of more than three decades of Professor Srinivas must have stood in good stead.

I am sure that the book will be received by the scholars and students alike.

New Delhi
September 2018

Vempaty Kutumba Sastry
President, International Association
of Sanskrit Studies

Preface

The preset work contains a collection of twelve essays on different aspects of Indian philosophy written over a period of time. Some of these essays were presented in the national and international seminars. The themes of these essays are categorized into three different areas. Under the first category, the subjects like Indian philosophy, Engaged Buddhism, and Comparative philosophy are discussed. By and large, they explain how the subject-matters of these areas of inquiry can be approached and understood. Under the second category, the philosophies of Yoga, Śrī Rāmānuja, and Sri Aurobindo are discussed with a view to present the most distinctive features of their philosophical doctrines. Under the third category, the specific themes such as the debate between the Buddhists and the Advaitins concerning the originality of their metaphysical doctrines, space and time as conceived in Mīmāṁsā, the nature of I-consciousness as interpreted by P.T. Raju, the possibility of self-knowledge, the various Indian theories of meaning, and the other in Indian philosophy are discussed. However, one may find connectivity among all these essays as one cannot strictly compartmentalize Indian philosophy into neat divisions like metaphysics, epistemology, logic, psychology, ethics, and religion for they are interrelated. Ultimately, the aim of this work is to show the richness of Indian philosophy in terms of its metaphysical, epistemological, logical, semantical, psychological, ethical, and religious aspects. The arguments and counterarguments to prove one's philosophical standpoint reign supreme in the classical Indian philosophical tradition. Although it is often interpreted by the writers on Indian philosophy that the ultimate goal of Indian philosophy is to attain liberation, yet one does not miss the importance given by the Indian philosophers to day-to-day problems of life. For them, the problems of life are nothing but the problems of philosophy. The issues ranging from ordinary (mundane) to extraordinary (extramundane) levels of human life got equal weightage in the philosophical discussions of the various systems of Indian philosophy. At the ordinary level of human life, science, polity, morality, aesthetics, psychology and religion dominate the philosophical discussions. At the extraordinary level of human life, it is natural that a spiritual aspirant tries to transcend the limits of the empirical world through the practice of a particular spiritual discipline that suits his or her organic constitution. Therefore, one has to pass through the social level to reach the spiritual level. All our arguments and counterarguments to prove a particular philosophical standpoint at the social level disappear once we transcend it to attain the spiritual level. Thus both organic and hyper-organic levels are inbuilt in human beings. It is left to the individual whether to transcend his or her organic level of existence to achieve the spiritual heights. But the classical Indian philosophers never preached that the social life of the individuals has to be ignored or neglected. The *puruṣārthas, dharma, artha, kāma* and *mokṣa,* clearly vindicate that the first three of them are restricted to the empirical level of existence, and the fourth one belongs to trans-empirical level.

I would be failing in my duty if I do not acknowledge my deep sense of gratitude to the following people. My association with the great minds like Prof. K. Satchidananda Murty, Prof. S.S. Barlingay, Prof. R. Balasubramanian, Prof. T.B. Siddalingaiah, Prof. Rama Rao Pappu, Prof. V. Kutumba Sastry enriched my understanding of Indian philosophy. Also, the talks delivered by Dr. V. Ananda Reddy (SACAR) on Sri Aurobindo enabled me understand the intricacies of his integral philosophy. Apart from this, the constant encouragement and support I received from my wife Ragini, and my friends Prof. Clement S. Lourdes, who designed the cover page for this book, Prof. C.S. Radhakrishnan, Prof. C. K. Ramaiah, and Prof. A. Subramanyam Raju, cannot be forgotten.

Introduction

The true ontological Being is the God of the Exodus and ahamasmi (I-Am) of the Vedānta. In India the highest ontological developments are found in the Vedānta.

– **P.T. Raju**

Often one wonders whether Indian philosophy is synonymous with Hindu philosophy. As aptly held by S.C. Chatterjee and D.M. Datta in their popular work *An Introduction to Indian Philosophy* (1930), this may be so if the expression 'Hindu' is taken in its geographical sense of 'Indian'.If the expression 'Hindu' refers to any religious faith, then the expressions 'Hindu' and 'Indian' are not synonymous for there are philosophies of Cārvāka, Jainism, and Buddhism that are part and parcel of Indian philosophy, but cannot be brought under Hindu philosophy. In other words, Indian philosophy represents the philosophies that are native to Indian soil. Indian philosophy is one of the oldest of oriental philosophies that can be traced back to the Vedic times. It is an ocean by itself. To churn this ocean to know the treasures hidden in it one single life is not enough. One has to take several births and rebirths. Of course, we have our own speculations about the Vedic period. The historians roughly fixed it between 4000 BCE to 700 CE. Although the Veda was originally regarded as a single compendium, its codification into four important Vedas—Ṛg, Yajur, Sāma and Atharva by Krişṇa DvaipāyanaVyāsa indicates that the Vedic literature addressed the curious questions concerning philosophy of life and spirit. The questions 'how? what? and with what?' are asked wherein human agency is involved. But, when these questions are applied to natural agency it is easy to assume that the involvement of personal forces cannot be ruled out. These personal forces are none other than the 'super humans' or the gods. Each god as a super person is responsible for some activity or the other. Once humans know that the gods are responsible for certain natural activities then they started worshipping them to control nature in their favour. Thus the vital questions concerning natural activities found their answers. This is the reason why the major portions of the Vedas are devoted to rituals and sacrifices.

There were seers who did not really relish the idea that religion would be the right way of understanding and controlling the nature and humans. Being the seekers of wisdom (*dārśaniks*), these seers went beyond the gods as sources of these natural activities and recognized an eternal and immutable cosmic order called *Ṛta.*As an eternal law, *Ṛta* controlled the activities of nature as well as humans. However, it is in the *Upaniṣads*, the end portions of the Veda, one comes across the real philosophical wisdom. The first three parts of the Vedas (*Saṁhitas, Brāhmaṇas* and *Āraṇyakas*), by and large, have religious orientation. A thorough cognitive inquiry into the workings of nature and humans' place in nature is undertaken in the *Upaniṣads*. This is the real spirit of philosophy as far as the classical Indian philosophical tradition is concerned.

The epic period is estimated between 1000 BCE-200 CE. The Vedic literature being highly precious and sacrosanct was not freely accessible to all, but only to those who were eligible to receive it. Hence the instruction was made strictly oral in nature. But there was a need for transmitting the Vedic knowledge in its diluted form for the public consumption. The great epics like the *Mahābhārata* and the *Rāmāyaṇa* served the purpose by disseminating the quintessence of the Vedic literature through folklore. The interesting feature of the epic the *Mahābhārata* is that it laid down certain rules of conduct of life. It is treated as a handbook of rules of life in all its dimensions that include religion, philosophy, polity, society, and medicine. The most important part of the *Mahābhārata* is the *Bhagavad-gītā,* which received universal acclaim for propagating the philosophy of activism. In the *Gītā* one comes across a detailed discussion on the nature of human being and universe. The prescription of the *Gītā* to humankind in terms of *niṣkāma-karma* is something unique. Although the *Rāmāyaṇa* is centered around the great king of Ayodhya, Śrī Rāma, it conveys the message of the ideals of womanhood and manhood by narrating the life stories of Sīta and her ideal husband Śrī Rāma. This epic also prescribes the ideals to be practiced by every individual for oneself as well as for the welfare of society in general.

During the epic period there appeared treatises on righteousness and justice (*Dharma-śāstras*). These compilations were chiefly meant to regulate individual human conduct as well as societal conduct in general. *Artha-śāstra* of Kautilya, *Manu-dharma-śāstra* of Manu, *Yājňavalkya-smriti* of Yājňavalkya, *Kāma-sūtra* of Vātsāyana were basically concerned with the way in which we ought to live as social individuals. The need for means of life is discussed in the *Artha-śāstra,* and the role and duties of a King for the purpose of institutional governance is discussed in *Manu-dharma-śāstra.* The justice and order in individual's life is discussed in *Yājňavalkya-smriti*. The *Kāma-sūtra* of Vātsāyana deals with science of erotics. Also, the various systems of philosophy started taking shape during the epic period but were not given much importance until the end of the epic period. It seems that there were references to some of the systems of philosophy even in the epic the *Mahābhārata.*

The beginning of the various philosophical systems was the end of epic period. These philosophical systems offered rational explanations concerning the nature of the world and place and role of humans in it. The philosophical wisdom of the ancient Indian philosophers is mirrored in this aphoristic style of writing. The *sūtras* or aphorisms of Cārvāka, Jainism, and Buddhism are termed as heterodox (*nāstika*) for they did not owe any allegiance to the Vedic authority. But the *sūtras* or aphorisms of Nyāya-Vaiśeṣika, Sāṅkhya-Yoga, Mīmāṁsā-Vedānta are called orthodox (*āstika*) for their allegiance to the Vedic authority. However, it is something remarkable that the development of Indian philosophy in general is attributed to the commentarial tradition. The peculiar thing that one notices here in the commentarial tradition is that the views of the various schools of thought are learnt before they are criticized. A philosopher has to first understand the philosophical position of his opponent before he arrives at his own theory. This is technically called prior view (*pūrvapakṣa*). Then it is followed by criticism (*khaṅdana*). The final position arrived at by the philosopher is called the conclusion (*siddhānta* or *uttarapakṣa*). In fact, the exposition of any system given by its critic as prior view is clearer than that is given by its own exponent.

In fact, the period of commentaries is traced back to 4th century CE. The great seers and *ācāryas* relentlessly worked on the *sūtras* of the various schools to examine and interpret them in their own perspective. The major commentaries on Akṣapāda Gotama's Nyāya aphorisms were written by Vātsāyana, Udyotakara, and Vācaspati Miśra. The commentary on Kanāda's Vaiśeṣika aphorisms was written by Praśastapāda. The commentary on Kapila's Sāṅkhya aphorisms was written by Īśvarakriṣṇa. The commentary on Patañjali's Yoga aphorisms was written by Vyāsa. The commentary on Jaimini's Mīmāṁsā aphorisms was written by Śabara. Later on the commentaries on Bādarāyaṇa's aphorisms of Brahma were written by Śaṅkara, Śrī Rāmānuja, and Madhva. Of course, there was no end for commentarial tradition. A long list of commentaries is available for detailed analysis. Commentaries on these commentaries were also written by the various scholars exhibiting the argumentative skills of Indian philosophers. The commentarial period gradually paved the way for renaissance.

The period of Indian renaissance basically started in the early 19th century unlike the Western one. The influence of Western ideas on Indian philosophers led to novel interpretation of the classical texts. The re-examination of the various Indian philosophical traditions resulted in a new outlook and orientation towards the fundamental philosophical issues that are nothing but the issues concerning human life. The issues concerning human life are both mundane and extra-mundane. Soteriology, excepting in the philosophy of Cārvāka, finds its due place in the philosophical discussions of classical as well as contemporary Indian philosophers. Thus one finds continuity in the tradition as something elastic rather than static.

Many people are of the opinion that Indian philosophy is spiritual, hence it is not practical. But it is other way round. Its emphasis on the self-realization as the highest value of humans often seen as an attempt to realize the spiritual goal. However, in order to achieve this spiritual goal one needs to pass through his/her social responsibilities as a moral agent. Bypassing one's social responsibilities as a moral agent may hinder one's spiritual growth. Thus there is a link between one's social responsibilities and spiritual growth. In this sense one can say that Indian philosophy is highly pragmatic. The central doctrines of Indian philosophy are the outcome of the experiential encounters of the great sages and seers. They are not speculative as many think. In fact, these doctrines are aimed at solving the basic problems of human life. The problems of human life, their reasons and causes are understood through personal encounters in order to make human life as comfortable as possible. The comfort is not viewed in terms of quantity, but in terms of quality of life enjoyed by the individuals. Although riches are important, they are not the sufficient condition for qualitative life. Many do not know this truth. The great Kings and Queens in spite of their riches encountered suffering in their lives. Happiness cannot be bought. It can only be experienced through right mindfulness.

Of course, speculative understanding of the natural forces is also necessary for perfecting one's own life. We need to distinguish between 'what is the case' and 'what ought to be the case'. Without understanding such a distinction one cannot see meaning and purpose of human life. If everything has to happen the way in which it is to happen then what is the role of humans as moral agents. This is where philosophy of action contributes to the quality of life. The actions based on conscience, and mere conscious actions are different. The former have intrinsic worth whereas the latter have mere extrinsic worth. But one should not forget that the actions of conscience necessarily involve consciousness.

The pragmatic worth of classical Indian philosophy is manifold. It not only takes into consideration the highest goal to be achieved by humans but also reminds them of their social responsibilities. The Indian renaissance movements, by and large, have taken a middle path wherein both material and spiritual dimensions of human life are given equal importance. The material dimension always stressed the importance of scientific temper (rationality) and moral autonomy (freedom). In the absence of scientific temper and moral autonomy material progress is not possible. The incidental sciences for the betterment of society are encouraged and patronized. The cultural history of India is a testimony to this fact. The spiritual dimension on the other hand reminds us that there is something more to achieve in human life. As reflective individuals we know the significance of spiritual form of life. It is a well-known fact that of all births human birth is so precious for humans alone are capable of introspection.

Therefore, while discharging our social responsibilities as moral agents we must also think of spiritual progress of society in general. Philanthropy, charity, adherence to truth, sense of responsibility, loyalty, and many more become part of our spiritual life. The moral agents not only act for themselves but also act for the welfare of the others. Thus 'the other' gains significance in Indian philosophy.

The duties of individuals are prescribed according to their caliber. The role of *brāhmins, kṣatriyas, vysyās* and *sūdras* is well defined for the maintenance of social order. This classification is mainly intended to promote division of labour for the harmonious function of society. *Brāhmins* are expected to advise and educate both the rulers and the ruled. According to the classical Indian tradition, they are endowed with *satvaguṇa*. The *kṣatriyas* are guardians of the territory (state) and the citizens of the territory. They are brave and courageous for they possess *rajoguṇa*. The *vysyās* have a mixed bag of both. The *sūdras* possess *tamoguṇa*. Therefore, they are expected to do all the menial jobs as they lack independent initiative. However, all the four are very important for a balanced welfare society. In a way this division of labour categories people on the basis of their inner talents or capabilities. One can excel in any field depending upon one's caliber. There are evidences in the *purāṇas* that people belonging to different *varṇas* performed different roles. The profession of any individual is decided by his natural caliber, temperament, and disposition, but not by his birth in a particular *jāti*. The social stratification of classes is essential for better social organization. Thus equal opportunities are given to the individuals depending upon their natural talents.

Also, there are stages of life (*āśrama-dharmas*) imposed on the individuals belonging to first three classes. They are: *brahmacarya, gṛhastha, vānaprastha,* and *sannyasa*. An individual is supposed to perform certain duties in each of the *āśramas*. In the first stage an individual is expected to learn the essence of the Vedas from a competent guru. Having accomplished the knowledge of the Vedas in accordance with the rules one can move to the stage of *gṛhastha*. As a married man he has to fulfil his obligations towards his family and society. In fact, both husband and wife have equal responsibilities As a *gṛhastha* one has to repay his debts to the seers and teachers for learning what ought to be preserved in terms of knowledge, parents and ancestors for providing an opportunity for progeny, and to gods for providing a gift of life in this world. Only after fulfilling one's obligations to his family and society one is allowed to devote himself for meditation and concentration. One has to renounce his family and other mundane comforts in order to meditate in the forests. Finally one becomes a wondering monk (*sannyāsi*), who is considered to be a realized soul while alive. Such a state is technically called *jīvanmukti.*

The classical Indian philosophy also suggested certain goals of human life (*puruṣārthas*). These goals of human life clearly vindicate that social life of individuals is as important as their spiritual attainment. Unless one discharges one's social commitments one cannot really aspire for spiritual attainment. The *puruṣārthas* are: *dharma, artha, kāma,* and *mokṣa. Dharma* represents righteousness and is thus an over arching principle that regulates the lower values *artha* and *kāma.* Everyone desires to enjoy life. However, one should not exceed one's limits of enjoyment by amassing the wealth (*artha*) and indulging in sensuous pleasures (*kāma*). A qualitatively good life is defined in terms of these goals or values. Every individual as a moral agent has to balance one's material and spiritual needs. The imbalance in any society is due to non-adherence to *dharma.* It is *dharma* that evokes in every one of us a sense of contentment. The uncontended life is miserable. The fourth goal or value *mokṣa* is of utmost importance. It is not necessary that everyone aspires for this goal. It only aims at complete freedom from rebirth. One who does not seek *mokṣa* has to undergo the cycle of births and rebirths. There is no end for such process unless one gets liberated from the cycle births and rebirths. The classical Indian philosophers have suggested three *mārgas*, namely, *jñāna-mārga, karma-mārga,* and *bhakti-mārga* to attain liberation. Each of these *mārgas* is prescribed to the individuals depending upon their temperament which is regulated by the various permutations and combinations of *sattva, rajas* and *tamas*. In fact, the principles of classical Indian social philosophy are based on the above said *varṇa-dharmas* and *āśrama-dharmas.*

The contemporary Indian philosophy is basically a movement of revivalism in which the fundamental tenets of classical Indian philosophy are recast to suit the needs of modern society. The contemporary philosophers like Swami Vivekananda, Rabindranath Tagore, Mahatma Gandhi, Sri Aurobindo, J. Krishnamurti, S.Radhakrishnan, Krishna Chandra Battacharya and others held that proper philosophy of life can be built up on the values that are essentially human. Thus they did not deviate from the classical Indian philosophical values. We come across in their writings the distinction between the concern of philosophy and the ideal of philosophical thinking. The concern of philosophy is to tackle the existential problems of the individuals living in different life-situations. Thus the needs of man and society become the primary concerns of philosophy. But the ideal of philosophical thinking makes us realize that at one point of time we have to transcend the limitations of the empirical world to attain absolute freedom. This is the ultimate goal of human life. The concern of philosophy makes us motivated individuals to face the various life-situations. By cultivating human values one cannot only lead a pious life that is worth emulation, but can also contribute to build a society where there is peace, and social harmony. This message is reflected in the writings of contemporary Indian philosophers.

K. Srinivas
Pondicherry

June 2018

1

Reunderstanding Indian Philosophy: Some Reflections of S.S. Barlingay

Introduction

S.S. Barlingay's posthumous publication *Reunderstanding Indian Philosophy* (1998) is an interesting work published in recent times which enables a keen student of Indian philosophy to get into its structural depths. Long before him the scholars such as S. Radhakrishnan, S.N. Dasgupta, M. Hiriyanna, P.T.Raju, S.C. Chatterjee and D.M. Datta, N.V. Banerjee, C.D. Sharma published their works on Indian philosophy and are also credited with disseminating the Indian wisdom to the Westerners. This does not mean that any work on Indian philosophy which was attempted thereafter is of less significance for the readers. Barlingay's *Reunderstanding Indian Philosophy* is a vindication of this fact. The prefix of the title 'Reunderstanding' clearly brings out the intention of the author. His relook at Indian philosophy is prompted by two fundamental questions. They are: (1) Is Indian philosophy determined by any geographical boundaries? (2) Is it the outcome of certain cultural patterns of the society? Barlingay's firm conviction that 'philosophy is philosophizing' is the outcome of his rigorous training in analytical tradition under Gilbert Ryle, one of the most influential analysts of his time. The art of philosophizing is neither Indian nor Western. It knows no geographical boundaries. Indian philosophy, according to Barlingay is a 'transferred epithet'. It can at best be called philosophy advocated by Indians. An attempt is made in this paper to show how Barlingay approached the concepts of Indian philosophy with a new vision. It is evident, according to Barlingay, that the philosophy developed in the post Renaissance Europe has taken two dimensions, namely, rationalism and empiricism. The philosophers, who belonged to either of these two camps, expressed their own views independently. Similar is the case with the Vedāntic tradition of India. In the 19th century the followers of Hegel called philosophy a system. Such a view, holds Barlingay, might have affected the Indian philosophical horizons also. The philosophies of India are somehow reduced to systems. The negative impact of such an exercise is that the systems are never allowed to grow independently. A system, in other words, becomes completely windowless and becomes a Leibnitzian monad. Neither philosophy nor science is a closed system, according to Barlingay. But there is no end for human reason. Even a system is a product of rational construction. He admits that he always looked at the writings of the great Indian philosophers with a critical eye, but it has a positive outlook. Therefore, Barlingay claims that his essays in the present work have a tone of scepticism.

What is Indian Philosophy?

Barlingay questions: In what way Indian philosophy is Indian? Is it something completely different from the rest of the philosophies? There is no doubt that some may think so. If that were the case just as different types of plants grow in different places, different philosophies grow in different regions. Thus each brand of philosophy makes an organic whole by itself. Such an interpretation provides us with an understanding that there are many philosophies. Every philosophy arises out of specific need(s) and aptitude of a given society. Another interpretation is that the distinction between Indian and Western need not be drawn on the lines of logical pattern that they exhibit, but are derived from the cultural patterns that they exhibit. This results in the view that there could be varities of philosophy in cultural pattern and also similarities of philosophy in different cultural patterns. Further he holds that there is yet another way of understanding Indian philosophy in the sense that it is the philosophy expounded by Indian philosophers. To quote him in the context: "'Indian' in such a case would not be an adjective of philosophy but would be a case of transferred epithet in as much as it would qualify the writers and not their thought."[1] Barlingay is of firm conviction that when we talk of Indian philosophy we have largely understood it in this sense. However, he does not ignore other two usages too. For my part, I believe that Indian philosophy is necessarily Indian for it is the philosophy that reflects the thinking, living, and feeling of its people. Although a philosopher of India might attempt to write something about British or German or French philosophies, but he would never be called a British philosopher, a German philosopher, a French philosopher. There is also a possibility that he may not know anything of his native philosophy. One finds many such cases in India. For instance, the notions such as 'Brahman', 'Ātman' are necessarily Indian. At best one can draw parallels between similar notions existing in other philosophies that exist outside Indian philosophy.

Sāṁkhya Concepts

Coming to classical Indian philosophies, Barlingay observes that they are treated as systems. He raises certain pertinent questions concerning the status of a system. What is so systematic about them? Are they derived from common axioms? Does each system have its own axioms or postulates? He begins by saying that man's attempt to understand reality or the world results in the act of philosophizing. Such an exercise is epistemic in nature. In that one may try to understand oneself as well as other selves too. Man's understanding of concept of philosophy involves either introspection or retrospection of one's own experiences. Therefore, Indian philosophical systems "must be understood against the anthropological background, and their basic nature must be epistemological."[2] The common assumptions of all the Indian philosophical systems, according to Barlingay, are as follows:

1. There is a world which exists in its own right.
2. There is a knower who is a part of this world, yet treated as a separate entity from the world.
3. The knower can know this world.[3]

Apart from the above said presuppositions, each philosophical system may add up something more to suit its metaphysics in order to be distinguished from the other systems in terms of its subject-matter. This is evident from the systems such as Vedānta, Sāṁkhya, and Vaiśeşika. These systems made an attempt to inquire into the notions such as real, reality, and universe. Advaita of Śaṅkara is more confined to *brahma-jijñāsa,* Viaśeşika to the number of *padārthas*, and Sāṁkhya to the classification of ultimate reality into *prakṛti* and *puruṣa.* Barlingay tries to show the similarity between the propositions that there is *prakṛti* and that there is matter. But they mean differently when analysed. If *prakṛti* represents the concrete world, matter is viewed as a common element in every thing that is existing. However, Barlingay points out that the notion of *prakṛti* as projected by Sāṁkhya is found wanting in many respects. His understanding of *prakṛti* results in the following four models:

1. *Prakṛti* is a sum total of concrete reality except human beings as self-conscious living beings.
2. Both *prakṛti* and *puruṣa* can be viewed as the result of conceptual division of the total reality into unconscious and conscious existents. Thus *prakṛti* is abstracted from the unconscious existents.
3. *Puruṣa* is the conscious element and *prakṛti* is regarded as a concrete entity consisting of all things in the world including the bodies of living things.
4. It is possible to think that *prakṛti* being concrete is one, and there exists a disembodied consciousness as a logical abstraction. But it is possible to think that *prakṛti* is inseparably connected with consciousness as a special variety resulting in multiple persons and each person is a unique particular. [4]

What Barlingay shows in the above analysis of Sāṁkhya is that although the metaphysical presuppositions of each system serve as axioms of that system, yet there is a possibility to derive many models from the same set of axioms. Thus the system becomes more open than closed.

Further, Śaṅkara's critique of Sāṁkhya dualism is based on the view that the division of reality into *prakṛti* and *puruṣa* reduces these categories into two abstractions. The former is considered to be non-vital, yet active; and the latter is vital, but non-active. But abstractions cannot be realities. Barlingay opines that majority of the problems in Indian philosophy arise because we have a tendency to regard epistemological or linguistic phenomenon as a copy of something, and that something 'is'. Something 'is' because it exists.[5] But we fail to notice that the word 'is' also used along with abstractions and words in language. When someone says this is my experience certainly his experience 'is'. But this 'is-ness', asserts Barlingay, is not the same as the 'is-ness' of things. If this distinction between 'is-ness' is not taken care of then a linguistic or epistemic dualism may turn out to be metaphysical or physical dualism. This is precisely what happened when *prakṛti* and *puruṣa* are treated in Sāṁkhya. The following illustration might help us understand this problem better. Of course we do distinguish between something without consciousness and the consciousness. In a living body we distinguish the body from its consciousness. In other words, both are characterized by 'is-ness'. But all forms of bodies, living, dead or any other form, possess 'is-ness'. Similarly, even consciousness is also characterized by 'is-ness'. Although it is not a practice to hold that even 'is-ness' also is, or characterized by 'is-ness'. Such a use of 'is-ness' leads to infinite regress. One should not forget the 'is-ness' of consciousness is similar to that of 'is-ness' of is. Similarly, *puruṣa* or consciousness in metaphysics need not be a separate entity from *prakṛti* although they appear to be different in expression. The linguistic realities do not represent metaphysical realities. Barlingay makes this point intelligible by the following analysis. The relation between *prakṛti* and *puruṣa* can be explained in the following way. Linguistically we hold that *puruṣa* is opposed to *prakṛti* as conscient. If *puruṣa* is the name given to totality of the functions, which is otherwise known as consciousness, then there is meaning in saying that *prakṛti* is non-conscient. However, action is not the function of consciousness alone, for it requires direction from something called will or intention. But the very basis of any action is the movement and that is certainly not a part of intelligence, consciousness or will. In that sense it is only the *prakṛti* that is the doer and *puruṣa* is nothing to do with action.[6]

Further Barlingay has his reservations with regard to the use the expression '*guṇas*' to represent *sattva, rajas and tamas*. If *guṇas* are qualities, then they are *dravytva, snehatva,* etc. But Sāṁkhya uses *guṇas* as constituent parts which are inseparable from *prakṛti*. These three constituent elements make the whole called *prakṛti*. However, there arises a misunderstanding when we treat them as physical parts of *prakṛti.* But they are not; and can only be seen as characteristics of *prakrti.*These characteristics of *prakṛti* cannot be treated like the *guṇas* of Vaiśeṣika for some of the qualities are external. *Sattva, rajas and tamas* being the constituent aspects (characteristics) of *prakṛti* cannot be external to it. They are also not the functions of *prakṛti* for we cannot say in our ordinary language that there is *sattva*. But we can say that there is consciousness. What Barlingay suggests us here is that we need to distinguish between a thing and its function, a thing and its parts, a thing and its separable qualities, a thing and its inseparable characteristics, a thing and a concept of thing before we undertake any philosophical position.

Coming to the origin and the explanation of the universe, since the time of Plato two questions, according to Barlingay, preoccupied our minds. They are: (1) What is the cause of origin and genesis of the universe? (2) What is the explanation of the universe? Although the nature of these two questions is different, we tend to confuse one with the other from time to time. These questions, strictly speaking, refer to two different enquiries. The first one is concerned with the temporality of the universe in that we are concerned with how the universe originated from a thing or things. The second question enquires about the classification of categories of one's experience by means of which the universe is explained. Almost all the schools of thought dealt with these two questions.

There is a debate with regard to the number of *padārthas.* Some say there are seven *padārthas* and others say nine *dravyas*. But for Naiyyāyikas even *pramāṇa* and *prameya* too are included in the category of *padārthas.* In philosophy, by and large, we are involved in the analysis of knowledge. But we tend to confuse it with causal explanation. This confusion is the result of the words that we use. Suppose we say that *prakṛti* is the cause of the world. The word 'cause' in Sanskrit is *kāraṇa.* Here in this context *kāraṇa* is understood as the temporal notion of 'cause'. But *kāraṇa* can also be understood in 'how-sense' and in the sense of purpose. Barlingay holds that most of the writers of the systems have interpreted *kāraṇa* in all the three senses resulting in three different kinds of enquiries that often make our understanding of Indian thought confusing.

Sāṁkhya theory of causation is popularly known as *satkāryavāda,* according to which effect pre-exists in the cause. *Prakṛti* is the primary cause that gives rise to evolutes due to its proximity to *puruṣa.* Barlingay is of the view that *puruṣa* is not the part of creation for it is not associated with it at any point of time. It is only a catalyst, hence called *kūṭastha.* Sāṁkhya has to maintain such a position in order to get rid of pain and misery. If *puruṣa* is associated with creation then it cannot get rid of pain and misery. Therefore, it must detach itself from pain and misery. But Barlingay notices some confusion here between *puruṣa* and individual. Individual suffers from pain and misery. If *puruṣa* is not a part of creation then how come there are so many of them. *Puruṣas* exist in individuals and experience pain. How did Sāṁkhya arrive at this model? It is also true that pain and misery do not belong to *prakṛti,* for it does not possess consciousness. One does not experience pain and pleasure without being conscious. Pain and misery do not arise without an object. In order to experience pain there must be identification of object with subject. In Sāṁkhya view it is the identification of *puruṣa* with *prakṛti.* But this false identification gives rise to pain and misery because *prakṛti* and *puruṣa* are opposite in nature. *Puruṣa* as a knower possess knowledge and is independent of the object of experience. Therefore, *puruṣa* is not affected by pain and misery.

Pratītya-Samutpāda, Sāmānya-lakṣaṇa, and Apoha in Buddhism

Those who are familiar with Buddhism do know the significance of *pratītya-samutpāda, sāmānya-lakṣana,* and *apoha* in its various doctrines. Buddhism starts with the view that there is nothing permanent and everything is constantly changing (*sarvam anityam*). This view is further established in the writings of later Buddhists such as Nāgārjuna, Diṅṅāga, Dharmakīrti, and Ratnakīrti. But this impermanence is of two types. They are: impermanence of life period and momentary impermanence. The first kind of impermanence is what is experienced and the second is what is presupposed by the first. Barlingay tries to highlight the difference between these two forms. The impermanence in life is what is immediately experienced in which there is a scope for permanent bodies, whereas the momentary experience provides us with the experience of flux or flow. The impermanence of life refers to phenomenal existence in which causation is possible and in the second form there is no scope for such things. These two forms of change (impermanence) can be characterized as macro and micro. At the macro level there is a meaning in saying that there is birth, life, death, beginning, continuity, end of thing and so on. This is typically the change in time. However, the change of time would be under the second category. When one is saying that there is change in everything one talks of change without any permanence. But at macro level change presupposes some permanence to entities or things in order to change.[7] In other words, the macro change presupposes micro change. There is a change within change. Buddhism aims to explain both these kinds of change and "also to explain the nature of causation as well as refute it."[8] *Prima facia,* it appears to be paradoxical, but Barlingay holds that there is no such contradiction involved in explaining causation and also to reject it. How does he proceed to show it? When human experience is explained from the point of view of anthropocentrism we need terms like causation, class, and inference as tools. All these tools are human constructs. But when one tries to understand reality without bringing in human understanding and human categories one has to show the limitations of such an understanding of reality which is dependent on the categories like causation, class, and inference. This is precisely what is done by the followers the Lord Buddha like Diňňāga, Dharmakīrti, Nāgārjuna. Often the limitations of these concepts are confused with something else as they are used.

Barlingay, for instance, takes up how the concept of *pratītya-samutpāda* is understood. Mrs. Rhys David and most of the writers on Buddhism following her interpret that *pratītya-samutpāda* upholds causation. Even Hiriyanna is not an exception to this interpretation, although he calls it the law of contingent causation in his *Outlines of Indian Philosophy*. Barlingay observes a fundamental flaw in this interpretation.If *pratītya-samutpāda* results in causation then it contradicts the main thesis of Buddhism that everything is impermanent. We are aware of the fact, reminds Barlingay, it is only through the Four Noble Truths the Buddha offered a solution to the problem of suffering. And suffering is attributed to the self only when we view it as the unity of apperception. If self is negated then its selfish impulses can also be negated. Since belief in the self-identity is the result of ignorance, if the latter is removed then the former vanishes. The first and foremost task of Buddhism then is to remove one continuous unity of self. Since everything is discrete and impermanent (*niraṇvaya*), the question of continuous self does not exist. We have the tendency of organising and arranging these discrete moments into one unity called self. As discussed above, Barlingay views impermanence at two levels, namely, macro and micro. We use the concepts such as causation, class, and inference only at the macro level. But contingency is something that cannot be excluded from both the levels. From the cosmic point of view there is no ontic reality which is responsible for these modifications (*vikalpas).* There are only moments. The Buddha could advocate such a view only by denying causation but not by advocating it. There are discrete units but they always remain discrete for there is no unifying force or reality above them. Barlingay advocates that *pratītya-samutpāda* is "in fact anything but the Law of Causation though it today it goes in the name of Law of Causation known as the Law of Dependent Origination."[9]

The counterpart of the Law of Dependent Origination at the micro level is the concept of *apoha,* which is linked up with the theory of meaning.According to this theory, there is no unity among particulars. It appears, observes Barlingay, the concept of *apoha* is the logical outcome of *pratītya-samutpāda.* What then is the relation between these two concepts? Of course, the notion of *apoha* leads us to many interrelated concepts such as the theory of classes- *vyāpti* and the notions such as *tādātmya,* and *tad-utpatti* ***and*** *svabhāva* and also to the notion of *svatva.* But Barlingay was chiefly interested in the relation between the theory of *pratītya-samutpāda* and the theory of *apoha.* Mrs. Rhys Davids interprets the theory of *pratītya-samutpāda* as that 'being present this becomes'. According to Hiriyanna it literally means 'arising in correlation with'. Thus, observes Barlingay, there is no causal nexus involved in the theory of *pratītya-samutpāda.* One does not find any causal necessity between one factor and another in *pratītya-samutpāda.* There is only a sequence. This sequence cannot be treated as a consequence. There is a series of movements and also the series of events. But one finds necessity only in the first order but not in the second order. To put it in the words of Barlingay: "What he (the Buddha) really meant was that there was something like the law of objective sequence, that time was irreversible. If this law was misunderstood for the law of causation, it will create all the muddle in Buddha's thesis."[10] Suffering or misery can be removed only when we separate the law of the moments from the law of the events. They are separated. The flow of events (*santāna*) is not denied by Buddhism, but there is an order in the flow in the sense that it moves only in one direction.

All our concepts like 'class or universal' are also human constructions (*vikalpa*), therefore they do not have any real ontological existence. They only exist in the sphere of language. Here Barlingay of the opinion that non-Buddhists and even some of the Buddhists did not grasp the distinction between *svalakşaṇa* and *sāmānya-lakşaṇa* which Buddhism aims at. In our causal language we speak of cause and effect relationship such as the seed as the cause and the sprout is the effect. But in Buddhist language it has to be put in the language of seed-continuum and sprout continuum. The seed at different time intervals such as $t_{1,}$ $t_{2,}$ $t_{3,}$ etc., is not the same. There is a continuous change in the seed which we do not observe. When the seed changes into sprout we see another change in the form of sprout. Therefore the seed at t_1 and the seed at t_2 are different. In other words, the seed at t_1 is the cause of the seed at $t_{2.}$ This is different from the seed as the cause of the sprout. Therefore there are two distinct ways of looking at causation here. Seed-seed cause-effect series is different from the seed-sprout cause-effect series. In fact, observes Barlingay, that the seed-seed cause-effect series only becomes a cause–effect series when we put it in cause-effect language which belongs to this empirical world. In other words, cause and effect relation belongs to *sāmānya-lakşaṇa.* This is what Barlingay terms as the 'onto-epistemic sphere' in which the entities that we perceive have some kind of duration or permanence, but they do not belong to the ontic sphere. As Barlingay maintains: "In the world of moments qua moment the cause and effect language is ineffective."[11] But when we allow cause-effect language in the world of momentariness (*kşaṇabhangavāda*) then we are bound to say that the seed at t_1 is the cause of the seed at $t_{2.}$ Even the word "seed" is inappropriate from the point of view of *kşaṇabhangavāda*. It is not the seed that undergoes change but some underlying 'ontological nucleus', and the seed is the name given to it. Therefore, the name 'seed' is only a human construct (*vikalpa*) and it belongs to *sāmānya-lakşaṇa.* For that matter, logic itself is the product of *vikalpa.* The concepts of logic, as rightly held by Barlingay, need some 'onto-epistemic' permanence.

In other words, such concepts attain the status of an universal. It is in this context he makes a distinction between ontological status and onto-epistemic status. The universal concepts have only the latter but not the former.

Coming to the concept of *jāti* or class character, it is to something to do with theory of meaning. Epistemologically there is a concept formation of *jāti*. Can this concept explain itself? Or does it require a philosophical explanation? Buddhists attempted to explain the concept of *jāti* in terms of *apoha.*According to this theory, the meaning of a thing is determined only by negating it and then by negating that negation. *Prima facia*, it appears to be a complicated process. This is what is otherwise known as *atadvyāvṛtti.* To put it succinctly, a thing is *tad*, and its negation is *atad* and the *vyāvṛtti* of *atad* will be the original form.[12] What made Buddhists to adopt such a complicated method? The prefix 'a' and the '*vyāvṛtti*' stand for the concept of difference. The *atadvyāvṛtti* or *apoha* stands for difference of difference. The concept of difference is referred to in Indian logic as *anyonyābhāva. Atadvyāvṛtti* is regarded as the law of double difference. If there is *A,* then its difference is shown in terms of its negation (~A). And that which is different from (~A) would be [~(~A)]. In other words, the same thing is symbolically shown in the following manner.

$$A \neq (\sim A), \text{ and } [\sim(\sim A)] \neq (\sim A), \text{ therefore, } [\sim(\sim A)] \equiv A.$$

The non-Buddhists, according to Barlingay, interpreted Buddhist *apoha* in terms of double negation. Some Buddhist logicians too interpreted it in the said form. Barlingay notices a fundamental flaw in this interpretation. According to him, "if the word a or *vyāvṛtti* stands for a difference then one is hardly able to conceive that, that which is different from the one that is different from the original is the original."[13] Such an argument does not stand for the law of double negation. Barlingay takes a different route altogether to show that if the original is ***A*** then that which is different from ***A*** can be ***B*** or ***C*** or ***D***. And then that which is different from ***B*** or ***C*** or ***D*** need not be ***A.*** It can also be ***C*** or ***D***. Nyāya-Vaiśeṣika logicians like Praśastapāda, Udayana refuted *apoha* on this ground. This criticism of Buddhist theory of *apoha,* according to Barlingay, is the result of its misinterpretation. If it is admitted that there are discrete particulars then in order to explain these particulars the concept of *jāti* arises through *sāmānya-*

lakṣṇa. Then we have knowledge of each particular. In the process of knowing a particular we also know some other particulars. Barlingay gives the example of a book. When we read a book we not only have the knowledge of the letters, but also of blanks and margins. In other words, we have the knowledge of each particular by eliminating the indistinct marginal knowledge of other particulars. This is in essence the theory of *apoha.* It literally means total exclusion (*vyāvṛtti*). This exclusion can be termed as difference. For instance, ***A*** is excluded from ***B*** is to say that ***B*** is excluded from ***A***. It also amounts to saying that ***A*** is different from ***B*** and ***B*** is different from ***A.*** This is here Barlingay cautions us not to get confused between the notion of difference (*bheda*) and the notion of exclusion *(apoha*). He offers an illustration through which he tries to explain away this distinction. Let us imagine that there is a world with 5 particulars although their number is innumerable. Let us say that there are ***A, B, C, D, E*** as particulars in the world. When one has the knowledge of ***A***, progressively one has also indistinct knowledge of other particulars (***B, C, D, E***). By eliminating this relatively indistinct knowledge out of the total gestalt that you are able to have the determinate knowledge of ***A***.[14]

Based on the above illustration Barlingay denounces the view that *apoha* can be treated as difference (*bheda*). He also rejects Nyāya-Vaiśeṣika view that it can be treated as *atyantābhāva.* Supposes to treat a thing ***A*** is different from a thing ***B*** is to have distinct knowledge of both. In other words, this difference (*bheda*) is shown in terms of non-existence of one thing in another (*anyonyābhāva*). Dharmakīrti introduced this term, according to Barlingay, as a technical term. In a universe where there are ***A, B, C, D, E,*** not only the set of ***B, C, D, E*** are different from ***A,*** but each one of them individually is different from ***A.*** But "this notion of difference is far removed from exclusion. ***A*** is different from ***B***. But something different from ***B*** does not indicate ***A*** for it can mean ***C*** or ***D*** or ***E*** or**...**"[15] This is to say the view that "***A*** is different from ***B***" does not suggest the total exclusion for ***A*** and ***B*** do not together exhaust the whole universe. This is further demonstrated by Barlingay with a suitable example. If elephant is different from horse, then a horse is not something that is different from elephant. It can also be different from a man, rat, cat and many other things.

Jīva and *Ajīva*

Jīva and *ajīva* are understood as two metaphysical categories of Jainism. The question that Barlingay raises here is: Is it a division or a category distinction or an abstraction? Do *jīva* and *ajīva* exclude each other? Our macroscopic experience of the world encounters both animate *(jīva)* and inanimate (*ajīva*) aspects. This can be treated as a fundamental division of the world. This division does not presuppose that life or *jīva* does not possess spatio-temporal aspects and material properties. In other words, one can certainly imagine objects with life and objects without life. But both consist of matter. This is to say both these forms of matter have some common characteristics or features which are spatio-temporal in nature. In other words, "whether something is living or non-living, it would primarily be material and located in space and would just be real, one that can be experienced."[16]

Our classification of experience at times becomes ambiguous, according to Barlingay, when we fail to distinguish the classification of real things from the classification of concepts. The latter involves abstraction. The confusion arises due to our treatment of concepts on par with things. The images of things and concepts succeed each other with such a quick succession resulting in wrong identity. This is precisely the mistake committed by Descartes. He thought extension and consciousness as substances instead of treating them as aspects of our experience. Thus he divided them into substances. Later on it was Spinoza who reduced these two substances into one and held that extension and consciousness are the attributes of the same substance. However, one can divide substance with extension into living and non-living substances. However minute is a living being it has extension. It may not be visible to our naked eye. The question that arises is: How can there be any *saṁyoga* or external relation between something which has extension and that which does not have extension? Jainism, along with many schools, might have noticed this difficulty they introduced the notions such as *liṅga-deha* and *kāraṇa-deha* were introduced. *Deha*, Barlingay observes, is with extension even if it is consciousness. This is precisely what is attempted by Jainism. There is only a division of matter into living and non-living forms. The physical division of world, Barlingay observes, is mistaken for abstraction, conceptualizing, and logicizing.

Further he maintains that any living being is conditioned by birth and death. Livingness or the state of consciousness is not found in the living being once it is declared dead. What is 'gone away' here is the life or consciousness. But it is only used in a metaphorical sense, according to Barlingay. Suppose someone says that a thing and the consciousness of a thing are two different things and they come into external contact with each other is incorrect. What Barlingay wishes to convey is that classifying things is of one kind and categorising things is of another kind. Division of things is possible only when they exist in their own right. But it is through abstraction we distinguish qualities or characteristics of things. These abstractions are neither in space nor in time.

Based on the above discussion one can say that Jaina division of *jīva* and *ajīva* is the division of *dravyas*. But each *dravya* has its own characteristics. Also, *dravya*s are within the space.

Śaṅkara on Prescriptive and Descriptive Sentences

Does Śaṅkara has his own philosophy of language to establish is thesis like *apoha or sphoṭa?*Like any other philosopher of language in the Indian tradition Śaṅkara also raised several important issues concerning the function of language and he provides a critiques of language to show that reality cannot be comprehended by language. However, he heavily draws his language by quoting profusely from the *Śruti* and the *Upaniṣads*. The reality is One and unqualified and the world in which we live has the status of *nāma* and *rūpa.* In order to demonstrate this point he made use of certain aspects of the theory of language. According to Jaimini, the Vedic sentences are prescriptive and imperative. This does not mean that Śaṅkara refuted the other functions of language such as commanding, and prescribing. Since the chief objective of Śaṅkara is a theoretical one, namely, how to know Brahman his emphasis on language is more descriptive than prescriptive. Excepting *śravaṇa, manana*, and *nididhyāsana,* Śaṅkara did not prescribe anything for a spiritual aspirant. He also challenged the *kṛyārthatva* of the entire Vedas. For Pūrva-Mīmāṁsā the entire Veda is seen as a prescriptive text which leads to the philosophy of action. This attitude of Pūrva-Mīmāṁsā sees no descriptive content in the Vedas. Śaṅkara did not agree with this position and makes use of the logia (*mahāvākyas*) such as '*aham brahmasmi*', '*sarvam khalu idam brahman*', '*tat tvam asi*', *so 'ham*' and so on. All these sentences are of different types and they need explanation for proper understanding. The purport of all these sentences is prescriptive. In order to prove his point Śaṅkara makes use of naïve name theory. We know a thing ostensively by naming it and by describing it. Brahman, for Śaṅkara, is such a one. Being a *bhūta vastu* Brahman is named or described or communicated only through language. The whole issues here is, according to Barlingay, Jaimini completely ignored the descriptive content of the Vedas while Śaṅkara, although he did not deny the prescriptive content in the Vedas, focussed on the descriptive content of the Vedas.

Further it must be noted that the sole objective of *Brahmasūtra* is to arrive at knowledge. This knowledge has to take a linguistic form and its form would be only descriptive and not prescriptive and injunctive.[17] Similarly, Barlingay tries to show that the expression '*brahma-jijňāsa*' should not be understood the way in which we understand the phrase 'the horse of a king'. In this case the king and horse are two different entities having independent existence of each other. There is a relation between two substantives here. On the contrary, the expression '*brahma-jijňāsa*' does not refer to any such relation. According to Barlingay, '*jijňāsa*' is only a grammatical substantive. In fact, it is only a verb. 'To know' like 'to desire' functions like a transitive verb. Thus, in the phrase '*brahma-jijňāsa*'the object of *jijňāsa* is only Brahman. Such an inquiry has to be descriptive.

Conclusion

It is evident from the above discussion that the art of philosophizing necessarily presupposes conceptual clarity. These concepts may belong to any realm of philosophy, but must be interpreted to make our understanding of a given text intelligible. This is the reason why Barlingay firmly held that the essence of philosophy is philosophizing. This art of philosophizing is a method, but not a subject-matter. Thus philosophy in this sense becomes universal for it defies all limitations (*upādhis*). This art of philosophizing is extended to all the concepts of experience encountered by individuals in their lives. It is true that, by and large, these experiences are conditioned by both physical and social environ in which an individual is situated. But we cannot simply set aside the schisms found in philosophy like Indian philosophy, Western philosophy and so on. Perhaps, Barlingay is of the opinion that these schisms are the outcome of the various cultural practices of the people all over the globe. For instance, the cultural practices of Jains may be different from those of Buddhists and Vedāntins. However, they are subsumed under the common head called Indian philosophy. This classification of cultures into the various systems of thought is arrived at by means of abstraction. Just as Husserl thought that philosophy is phenomenology, Barlingay is of the opinion that philosophy is philosophizing. In both the cases it is nothing but a method which is applied to various experiential phenomena. But one may disagree with Barlingay and claim that the essence of culture is philosophy. Even if it were so, one cannot rule out the role of conceptual analysis for better understanding of any given position. As Barlingay rightly observed, by and large, all our experiences require a linguistic portal. But there are some experiences that transcend it too. This may be the reason why earlier Wittgenstein held that: "Whereof one cannot speak thereof one must be silent."[18]

Also, one has to notice that our linguistic portal is ridden with certain systematically misleading expressions. In addition to that we commit category mistakes. In Aristotle's metaphysics, for instance, a condition is termed as cause. A condition is a human creation whereas cause is something natural. Similarly, the expression '*tādātmya*' is neither similarity nor identity. To be similar or identical is to posit the existence of at least two numerically different individuals. One can establish similarity and identity between them. But *tādātmya* is neither of them. It can be treated as 'sameness'. Brahman and Ātman in Advaita are neither similar nor identical but they are one and the same. In essence, Brahman is the same as Ātman. Further Barlingay made an attempt to show that physical or material division of things is not to be identified with classification of qualities. We classify the qualities of substance through the process of abstraction. But the physical division of things does not involve the process of abstraction. Misuse of concepts makes our understanding of a given subject opaque and blurred. All our arguments either in support of a position or its denial become inadequate and illogical when we fail to see the context in which a concept is used. No concept is a closed one for it throws ample scope for further interpretation.

Notes

1. S. S. Barlingay, *Reunderstanding Indian Philosophy*, New Delhi: D.K. Printworld, 1998, p. 16.
2. *Ibid.,* p. 17.
3. *Ibid.*
4. *Ibid.,* pp. 24-25.
5. *Ibid.,* p. 39.
6. *Ibid.,* p. 61
7. *Ibid.,* p. 60.
8. *Ibid.*
9. *Ibid.,* p. 62.
10. *Ibid.,* p. 64.
11. *Ibid.,* p. 66.
12. *Ibid.,* p. 70.
13. *Ibid.*
14. *Ibid.,* p. 71.
15. *Ibid.,* p. 72.
16. *Ibid.,* p. 144.
17. *Ibid.,* p. 219.
18. L. Wittgenstein, *Tractatus Logico-Philosophicus,* C.K. Ogden (trans.), London: RKP, 1981, p. 7.

2

Did Nāgārjuna's Mādhyamika Influence Gauḍapāda?

Introduction

It is believed by many Buddhist scholars that Nāgārjuna's *sūnyavāda* directly or indirectly influenced Gauḍapāda's philosophy. This is further substantiated by the argument that one finds lot of similarities between the philosophies of Nāgārjuna (2nd century AD) and Gauḍapāda (8th century AD). Chronologically speaking the former lived almost 600 years earlier than the latter. The seminal work of Nāgārjuna is *Mūlamādhyamakakārika;* and Gauḍapāda's *Māndūkyakārika* (*Gauḍapādakārika*) is supposed to be the first systematic treatise on Advaita Vedānta. The fundamental philosophical doctrine in Gauḍapāda's *Māndūkyakārika* is the doctrine of no-origination (*ajātivāda*). A detailed account of this doctrine is provided in the third chapter of his *Kārika.* According to this doctrine, there is no real creation (*jāti*) and the world of plurality is only an appearance. We often tend to mistake this appearance as real due to ignorance (*avidyā*). Similar views are found in the *Mūlamādhyamakakārika* of Nāgārjuna. An attempt is made in this essay to show the similarities between Nāgārjuna's *sūnyavāda* and Gauḍapāda's Advaita Vedānta.

Mādhyamika of Nāgārjuna

Mādhyamika school of Buddhism is known for its *sūnyavāda.*

The literal meaning of the term 'Mādhyamika' is "the follower of the middle path". It avoids all sorts of dogma and dualisms to follow the teachings of the Buddha in their true spirit. Chandrakīrti wrote a commentary on Nāgārjuna's *Mūlamādhyamakakārika* to elucidate the significance of the Doctrine of Dependent Origination (*pratītyasamutpāda*) as explained by the latter. Nāgārjuna's Mādhyamika avoids all forms of extremes such as eternalism and annihilationism, self and not-self, matter and spirit, body and soul, substance and process, unity and plurality, affirmation and denial, identity and difference and so on. It virtually treads the middle path.[1] Unlike the *ātmavādins,* who claim that reality is eternal and immutable, the *anātmavādins* hold that the ultimate reality is neither unchanging nor eternal but is a pure flux (*sūnya*).[2]

Nāgārjuna being a well-known dialectician and the seeds of his *Mādhyamika* are said to be found in the *Mahāyāna Śraddhotpāda Śāstra* of Aśvaghoṣa, the author of *Budhacarita.* This is translated as 'The Awakening Faith in the Mahāyāna'. However, a systematic exposition of the philosophy of Mādhyamika is attributed to Nāgārjuna, who is known for his penetrating intellect and extraordinary dialectical skill. The method, teaching, and the spirit of the philosophy of Mādhyamika is found in his *Mūlamādhyamakakārika.* Apart from Nāgārjuna, the other thinkers responsible for the promotion and dissemination of the philosophy of Mādhyamika are Chandrakīrti, Kumārajīva, and Śāntideva.

Insofar as the background of Indian philosophical tradition is concerned, in general the philosophical schools in India are divided into two important schools, namely, heterodox (*nāstika*) and orthodox (*āstika*). The former do not owe their alliagiance to the Vedic authority and the latter do. As mentioned elsewhere, the schools of Buddhism being one among the heterodox schools do not subscribe to the Vedic authority. Hence they do not believe in a substantial permanent self (Ātman). Hence they are popularly known as *anātmavādins*. The *ātmavādins* include Jainism, Nyāya-Vaiśeṣika, Sāṅkhya-Yoga, and Mīmāṁsā–Vedānta. Although Jainism is categorized under the heterodox systems, yet Jainism believes in rebirth and immortality of the self (Ātman). Thus these systems subscribe to eternalism. On the contrary, *anātmavādins* hold that the ultimate reality is devoid of unchanging and eternal entities. It is a pure flux. In fact, the distinction between *ātmavādins* and *anātmavādins* is akin to the distinction between the doctrines of the ancient Greek philosophers Parmenides and Heraclitus. The former held that the Reality is One and unchangeable and the later believed in the notion of impermanence (flux). This distinction is further carrie on to show that the *ātman* philosophers are the 'philosophers of identity', and the *anātman* ones are the 'philosophers of difference'. This distinction is further stretched to characterize these philosophical schools as the advocates of the two important doctrines, namely, 'the doctrine of One (monism)' and 'the doctrine of many (pluralism)'.

Nāgārjuna was basically concerned with the origin and nature of philosophies and philosophical conflicts. His approach to these issues is highly insightful. According to him, the doctrines of philosophy emerge due to man's unquenchable thirst for the real, the ultimate, the unconditioned, and the absolute. Viewing the world as something other than oneself man goes in search of the knowledge of the world. But knowledge always presupposes the relation between the knower and the known. Both the knower and the known together constitute the knowledge situation. In a way, knowledge is the means by means of which man tries to unite the self and the other. The quest for knowledge is nothing but the quest for being. In other words, man in his quest for knowing the world simply appropriates it to himself. Nāgārjuna first of all asks the following questions: 1.What is knowledge? 2. How is it generated? His answers to these questions bear testimony to his revolutionary insights of the Mādhyamika School. Knowledge has to be expressed through propositions, and the propositions constitute both the concepts and percepts. They are known as names (*nāma*) and forms (*rūpa*) respectively. Accordingly, the reality which philosophers infer from their knowledge of the world is only the reality of names and forms. This is only the phenomenal reality wherein names and forms are located in spatio-temporal matrix. Early Wittgenstein too held in his *Tractatus* that propositions alone constitute knowledge. Similarly, Kant held that propositions (judgments) are made up of concepts and percepts. But the reality in itself is not made up of names and forms. But in their quest for the real, philosophers tend to mistake the reality created out of names and forms for reality itself. Like the thirsty travelers in the desert, who cannot distinguish reality from illusion, the philosophers too do not distinguish the reality of names and forms from the reality itself. Thus man loses his way in the jungle of his own imaginative creation or construction (*vikalpa*). The failure to distinguish the reality of names and forms from the reality itself leads to suffering (*duhkha*). Each school in its quest for reality puts forth its doctrines and claims them to be absolutely true and valid, and condemns the doctrines of the other schools as false and irrational. Thus we create philosophies of dogmatism that lead us to unwarranted blind faith in certain dogmas. These dogmas further lead us to intolerance, opposition and conflict.

Now the question before Nāgārjuna is: Can one capture Reality through names and forms? The Mādhyamika answer to this question is negative. How does it substantiate its negative answer? The key is to be found in Mādhyamika's analysis of the nature of thought and knowledge. The thought, according to Mādhyamika, originates from and dependent on the polar nature of the concepts. Every concept is polar in that it derives its meaning from its opposite. This is not only the case with polar concepts such as 'big and small', 'hot and cold', 'light and dark', 'certain and uncertain', but with respect to all concepts. For instance, the concept 'chair' derives its meaning from the concept of 'non-chair'. It is through the logical operation of polar concepts, which constitute the polar nature of thinking, knowledge becomes intelligible. In the absence of polar concepts and polar nature of thinking, our language, thought, and knowledge are not possible at all. They simply vanish. Another important question raised by the Mādhyamika is: Is there a unique way in which concepts can be brought together in order to generate knowledge? The Mādhyamika answer to this question is negative. There is no unique way of relating concepts to each other. In fact, the way in which the concepts are related to each other is dependent on many considerations. The most important of them is the presuppositions of the given thinker or a system of philosophy. Therefore, it is impossible to demonstrate within a given system of reality the presuppositions of that system itself. Any attempt to demonstrate their validity within a given system leads to circularity for the simple reason that the demonstration has to employ the same concepts and categories which are presupposed by a system. This ends up in the fallacy of begging the question (*petitio principii*). Thus transcendental reductions, according to Mādhyamika, are circular and a lame exercise. Thus every claim to demonstrate the reality is bound to be dogmatic and every attempt to demonstrate truth of the claim circular.

The above discussion clearly shows that Mādhyamika upholds the view that concepts and conceptual systems are relative to each other, for no concept or a conceptual system can stand on its own. The truths derived from them are only relative and necessarily dependent upon those generated by other systems. Therefore no system can lay claim to absolute truth and validity. Thus the truths of each system are relative and partial. The theories of reality are mere conceptual constructions, and each one of them emphasizes on a particular aspect with a specific point of view. The advocates of each system forget the fact that their systems are necessarily dependent on other systems, including his/their opponent's, claim absolute truth and unconditional validity for their system and reject other systems as false. The reason for such an attitude is man's quest for the real, the absolute, the ultimate, and the unconditioned. Thus system builders cling to their own constructions of reality without realizing the fact that their clinging is due to ignorance which results from their ignorance to distinguish a view of reality from the reality itself. This ignorance is the source of suffering (*duhkha*). Nāgārjuna advises people to realize the relativity of their thought-constructions. The true philosophy, according to Mādhyamika, is that which liberates men from the shackles of ignorance. Therefore it must promote the dialectical consciousness of the limitations of our thought constructions of reality out of names (*nāma*) and forms (*rūpa*).

Freedom, according to Nāgārjuna, is that which liberates us from the relative thought-constructions of reality. Accordingly, we must realize the relativity of all views of reality. *Prajñā-pāramita,* the highest wisdom, intends to liberate us from the relative thought constructions of reality, and at the same time leads us to direct, non-perceptual, non-conceptual, intuitive insight into reality. *Prajñā,* thus, is perfect freedom and perfect peace.

The Dialectical Method of Nāgārjuna

To be consistent with its views, namely, the relativity of all views about reality, Mādhyamika does not propound or defend any theory or doctrine of its own. Accordingly, the technique adopted by Mādhyamika dialectic is *reduction ad absurdum* (*prasanga*). The technique is to state the thesis/view of the opponents by following the rules and principles laid down by them in order to show the self-contradictory nature of the thesis/view of the opponents. Since the advocates of the thesis/view seek freedom from the contradiction as a necessary condition for its truth, they have to withdraw their claim to the truth of their thesis/view. What is gathered from this is that the proponents of a thesis/view themselves realize their false construction of reality. It is also important to note here that, according to Mādhyamika, if the thesis ***A*** is proved to be self-contradictory, it does not mean its anti-thesis (non ***A***) is proved to be non self-contradictory. In this respect the method of Mādhyamika (*prasanga*) differs from the method of *reduction ad absurdum* as employed by the other philosophers.

Now we shall discuss the nature of causation, according to Nāgārjuna. In fact, there are two prominent theories of causation in Indian philosophy. They are: *satkāryavāda*, and *asatkāryavāda.* The former is the doctrine, according to which, the effect pre-exists in the cause, and the latter holds that the effect is something new and does not pre-exist in the cause. Sāṅkhya and Advaita Vedānta advocate *satkāryavāda*, and Nyāya-Vaiśeṣika, and the realist schools of Buddhism advocate *asatkāryavāda*. Nāgārjuna puts forth four possible alternatives concerning any concept. As regards causation, they are: 1. A thing arises out of itself, 2. A thing arsies out of a not-self, 3. A thing arises out of itself and not-self, 4. A thing arises neither out of itself nor out of a not-self. The first and second alternatives represent *satkāryavāda* and *asatkāryavāda* respectively. Let us examine this *catuṣkoti.*

As held by *satkāryavādins*, if the effect pre-exists in the cause, then the effect is identical with its cause. In other words, there is no distinction between the two. Consequently, it is meaningless to speak of causation, for causation is a relation between two events or things, and for it to be a genuine relation there must be a difference between cause and effect. Thus the stand of *satkāryavādins* leads to self-contradiction. Therefore, the thesis of *satkāryavādins* does not hold water. Coming to the thesis of *asatkāryavādins,* if effect is something totally new for it does not pre-exist in its cause, then it amounts to saying that they are two independent events. How can anyone establish causal link between them? How are they related to each other? Even if one constructs a relation between two independent events, it is difficult to establish that it is a causal one. In a way, to answer this is to beg the question. Any logical answer to this question must reveal us that what is to say one is the cause and the other is effect. If two events are distinguished as cause and effect, then we must give valid reasons for saying so. Further, if the effect is totally unrelated to the cause, then nothing can be produced from anything. Therefore, according to Nāgārjuna, the thesis that cause and effect are absolutely different is as self-contradictory as the thesis that cause and effect are identical with each other. Both the theories of causation have failed to realize that a relation has two functions. They are: unity and separation where they can be no unity, there can be no separation and vice-versa.

The third alternative is refuted on the ground that it is the combination of the first and the second. The view that the thing arises out of itself is absurd then the thesis that it arises out of a not-self is also absurd. Then it amounts to saying that it arises out of both itself and not-self is also absurd. The fourth alternative needs no refutation, for it abandons causation. In the similar fashion, Nāgārjuna analyses the relation between substance and its attributes. There are two conflicting views regarding the nature of substance and its attribute. According to one view, substance real and the attributes are not real, and according to the other vie attributes are real but not substance. Nāgārjuna asks the question that a substance is known through its attributes only, and without substance attributes cannot exist. In a way, substance and attributes are not the same and different. Even in this case, a dogmatic claims reality either to substance or to the attributes although both the categories are interdependent. It is evident from our experience that there cannot be attributes without substance. Similarly, we recognize substance only through its attributes. By saying so Nāgārjuna is not committed to saying that substance and attributes have absolute and ultimate existence. All that he wants to establish is that the existence (reality) of each is conditioned by the other. Thus their existence is only relative. Nāgārjuna cautions us not to mistake these relative entities for absolutes. He also subjects the other concepts such as 'existence and non-existence', 'self and not-self', 'unity and plurality', 'subject and object', 'rest and motion' to similar treatment. These concepts do not refer to any independent absolute entities in reality. Being mutually dependent concepts, they only signify relative existence.

Void-ness (*Sūnyata*)

It is shown above that Nāgārjuna refuted causation. Now the question that arises is: By denying causation is not Nāgārjuna denying the existence of the empirical world? Is he not an advocate of nihilism? It is a misconception to think that Nāgārjuna subscribes to nihilism. In fact, he is treading the middle path. According to Nāgārjuna, it is absurd to talk of reality being true or false. Reality simply 'is'. What does it mean? Denial of causation entails the denial of reality provided that reality is constituted by causes and effects. Unless and until this supposition is proved to be true, one cannot say that Nāgārjuna denied reality. What he aims at showing here is that reality is not constituted by causes and effects. It is not the import of Mādhyamika dialectic to deny the reality, but its intention is to show that the concepts of cause and effect do not have any absolute reference in reality. This is what Nāgārjuna meant when he said the concepts are empty and void (*sūnya*). It is also worth emphasizing here that the emptiness of concepts does not mean emptiness of reality. Of course, Nāgārjuna refers to reality as *sūnyata.* But his notion of *sūnyata* should not be interpreted in its ordinary sense. It is empty in the sense that it is devoid of all the concepts and categories through which we refer to the absolute. His reality being absolute, independent, and unconditional, it cannot be grasped by the instruments of reason.

Nāgārjuna maintains that some followers of the Buddha failed to understand his central teachings. The Doctrine of Dependent Origination (*pratītyasamutpāda*). Especially the followers of the realist schools of Buddhism, namely, the Sautrāntika and Vaibhāśika fell prey to ignorance, illusion, and dogmatism. Similarly, Yogācāra claimed exclusive reality to consciousness (*vijňāna*). All existents (*dharmas*) are devoid of their own being and are relative. Thus the relativity and *sūnyata* of Mādhyamika upholds the Doctrine of Dependent Origination.

Lower and Higher Truths

The Buddha, claims Nāgārjuna, taught us two truths, one concerning the world of phenomena, which is grasped though names and forms, and the other to reality as its is in itself, which is beyond all names and forms. The phenomenal world of names and forms is governed by the Doctrine of Dependent Origination. Any truth that is generated by a conceptual system is relative to and dependent upon other truths and systems. In the phenomenal world one cannot find absolute truth or truth of the absolutely real. The phenomenal truths reflect only our perceptual and conceptual experience. Therefore, Nāgārjuna calls them conventional, relative, mundane, and lower truths (*samvṛtti-satya*). In contrast to these relative or lower truths, there is an absolute, supra-mundane, unconditional, higher truth, which is beyond percepts and concepts, ineffable and defies all descriptions. This higher truth is called by Nāgārjuna the *pāramārtha-satya.*This truth is grasped by direct intuitive insight called *prajña.* In fact, the Buddha never entertained the questions of non-empirical type such as whether the world is eternal or non-eternal, finite or infinite, whether the soul is the same as or different from the body, whether or not one who attains *nirvāṇa* exists after death, and what *nirvāṇa* itself is. The Buddha's reason for keeping silent about these questions is that they cannot be comprehended by reason and sense-experience. If anyone attempts to answer these questions through names and forms, they result in confusion, ignorance and dogmatism.

The dogmatic opponents of Nāgārjuna, both ancient and modern, have labelled his dialectic as destructive and charged him with exhorting men to reject commonsense, science and philosophy as false and vain. Such a charge against Nāgārjuna's doctrine is totally uncalled for. He never marginalized the importance of commonsense, science, and philosophy in this phenomenal world. In fact, he always held that without reason and logic men cannot know anything in this phenomenal world. Nāgārjuna never undermined the importance of science, logic, philosophy and commonsense and their pragmatic worth. What he rejected is that their pretentions to reveal the nature of the real. He only suggested men to be cautious about the pretentions and illusions created by them. In this context let us say a few words about Nāgārjuna's most cryptic and bewildering utterance, that there is no difference between mundane existence and *nirvāṇa*. What he meant by this utterance is that mundane existence (*saṁsāra*) and *nirvāṇa* do not belong to two different ontological levels, but are one and the same reality looked at from two different standpoints, namely, the lower and the higher. The progressive movement from *saṁsāra* to *nirvāṇa* is epistemological but not ontological. When we rid ourselves of confusion, illusion, ignorance, dogmatism, and attachment to thought-constructions, *saṁsāra,* the evry world of our ordinary experience gets transformed into *nirvāṇa.* Like any other distinction, the distinction between *saṁsāra* and *nirvāṇa* is also relative. So *prajňa* is not only the power to experience the world so transformed, and the wisdom such experience brings about.

To sum up, *prajňa* is the highest wisdom as well as freedom from all attachments and illusions. Nāgārjuna maintains that one should not get oneself attached even to *sūnyata* or emptiness, relativity, *nirvāṇa,* or the Buddha himself. Clinging to anything as unconditioned reality results in illusion and suffering. Thus the Buddha's teachings find their clearest expression in the dialectic of Nāgārjuna. The philosophy of Mādhyamika represents the wisdom of the Buddha. As a matter of fact, the philosophy of Nāgārjuna has become the source of inspiration to both Tibetan and Zen forms of Buddhism.

Gauḍapāda's Strict Monism (Advaita)

Gauḍapāda's *Māṅdūkyakārika* provides a strict monistic doctrine after the *Upaniṣads*. Thus *Māṅdūkyakārika* assumes importance.[3] Even Śaṅkara admits that it is Gauḍapāda, but not the author of *Brahmasūtra,* Bādarāyaṇa, who revived the *Upaniṣadic* teachings.[4] Accordig to Dasgupta: "I believe that there is sufficient evidence in his *Kārakas* for thinking that he was possibly a Buddhist, and considered the that the teachings of the *Upaniṣads* tallied with those of Buddha."[5] Similarly, Hajima Nakamura held that there is a possibility that *Māṅdūkya Upaniṣad* itself is influenced by the *Sūnyavāda* of Nāgārjuna for the former's composition could be around 200 AD.[6] He argues that "the concept of the fourth realm (*caturtha*) was perhaps influenced by the *Sūnyata* of the early *Mahāyāna Sūtras* in the formation of the *Māṅdūkya.*[7] As interpreted earlier, Nāgārjuna held that Rality is beyond the four categories of thought (*catuṣkoṭi-vimirmukta*). Similarly,

Gauḍapāda held the view that only an ignorant person covers the Real with existence, non-existence, both and neither. These are the four categories of thought with which the Real is covered, but in reality the Real transcends ll the four categories of thought. One who realizes it becomes the omniscient real.[8] Gauḍapāda talks of creation only from the relative point of view. His doctrine of *ajātivāda* or no-origination which he discussed in the third chapter of his *Kārika* emphasized the fact that there is any *jāti* or real creation. The world of plurality is only an appearance. The appearance of the phenomenal world is due to *avidyā.* Brahman/Ātman is said to be the only Reality. To put it in the words of C.D. Sharma: "Negatively, it means that the world, being only an appearance, is in fact never create. Positively, it means that the Absolute, being self-existent, is never created (*aja*)."[9]

Concluding Remarks

It is beyond doubt that the evidence available shows that Gauḍapāda was influenced by Nāgārjuna when the latter held that origination from the absolutist point of view is an absurdity. Whatever exists from the perspective of other-dependent (*paratantra*) does not really exist from the absolutist point of view.[10] As a matter of fact, Gauḍapāda employed the discourse of Mādhyamika to explain the two levels of reality, namely, the empirical (*samvṛti*) and the trans-empirical (*pāramārtha*). He maintained that things exist empirically, but they do not have real existence from the absolute point of view. Gauḍapāda examined the various theories of evolution and rejected all those. From the absolute point of view, there is neither birth nor death, neither apperanace nor disappearance, neither production nor destruction, neither liberation nor bondage; there is neither the aspirant nor the liberated—this is the highest truth.[11] Gauḍapāda talked of creation only from the empirical standpoint. The unborn appears to be born only due to *avidyā.* It is the *avidyā* that makes One appear as many. He further provided a detailed account of the doctrine of no-origination (*ajāti*) by means of a dialectical critique of causation. He established *ajātivāda* by proving the falsity of the world through *Śruti.* The world is only an appearance of the non-dual eternal principle Brahman/Ātman.[12] In the fourth chapter, Gauḍapāda in nineteen *Kārikas* made it clear that the

Buddhists elucidated *jāti* by giving the following three arguments. They are as follows:

1. There is absence of energy in the cause to produce the effect (*asakti*).
2. There is absence of knowledge of any relation between cause and effect (*aparijňāna*).
3. There is incompatibility of order of succession (*karma-kopa*).

In the twenty second verse he conclude that nothing can originate either from itself or from other than itself; neither the real nor the unreal nor both real and unreal can be produced.[13] This view of Gauḍapāda echoes that of Nāgārjuna. What is eternal cannot be produced. Therefore, it is unborn (*aja*). It is called born only from the relative point of view. From the absolute point of view, it is indescribable for its nature cannot be grasped by ordinary intellect.[14] The two levels of reality of Gauḍapāda are same as the lower and the higher truths of Nāgārjuna.

Further, it can be noticed that certain expressions used by Nāgārjuna and the expressions used in the *Māňdūkya Upaniṣad* resemble a lot. The introductory remarks of Nāgārjuna in his *Mūlamādhyamakakārika* reveal that he equated Doctrine of Dependent Origination with "the cessation of the phenomena (*prapaňcopāsamana*) and as auspicious (*daiva*). In verse 7 of the *Māndūkya Upaniṣad, Tūriya-Ātman* is also treated in the similar fashion. It is mentioned in *the Upaniṣad:* "The fourth is ...where there is the cessation of the phenomenal world (*prapaňcopāsamana*), it is peaceful, auspicious, and non-dual. According to the Buddhist scholars, perhaps *Māňdūkya* is influenced by the *Mahāyāna*. It is interesting to note that the fourth chapter of the *Māňdūkyakāika* abandons the traditional *ātmavāda* of the orthodox Vedānta in favour of *anātmavāda*. It does not refer to Brahman/Ātman at all. There are references to not-self, *sūnyata*, and the non-differentiated consciousness which is the ultimate reality. In the same chapter Gauḍapāda used the Buddhist terminology in order to present his Advita Vedānta. Thus there is every reason to believe that Gauḍapāda's *Māňdūkyakārika* was influenced by the *Mahāyāna* Buddhism of Nāgārjuna. This claim is further substantiated by one of the renowned contemporary Buddhist philoosphers, T.R.V. Murti. According to him: "Gauḍapāda appears to us as the Brahmanical thinker boldly reformulating the *Upaniṣadic* ideal in the light of the Mādhyamika and Vijñānavāda dialectic. But there was more borrowing of techniques than tenet."[15] Gauḍapāda borrowed the seminal ideas from Mahāyāna Buddhism to suit his philosophical position, namely, the Advaitic perspective.

Notes

1. R. Puligandla, *Fundamentals of Indian Philosophy*, New Delhi: D.K. Printworld (P) Ltd., 1996, p. 81.
2. *Ibid.*, p. 82.
3. S.N. Dasgupta, *A History of Indian Philosophy*, Delhi: Motilal Banarsidass, 1997, Vol.1, p. 422.
4. *Ibid.*, p. 423.
5. *Ibid.*
6. Hajima Nakamura, *A History of Early Vedānta Philosophy*, Delhi: Motilal Banarsidass, 1983, pp. 30 & 42.
7. *Ibid.*, p. 34.
8. *Māṅdūkyakārika,* IV, 83-4.
9. C. D. Sharma, *A Critical Survey of Indian Philosophy*, Delhi: Motilal Banarsidass, 1988, p. 242.
10. *Māṅdūkyakārika,* IV, 73.
11. *Ibid.*, II, 32.
12. *Ibid.* II, 31-35; III.17-23; 27-31.
13. C. D. Sharma, *A Critical Survey of Indian Philosophy*, 1988, p. 242.
14. *Māṅdūkyakārika,* IV, 74.
15. T.R.V.Murti, *The Central Philosophy of Buddhism*, London: George Allen & Unwin, 1974, p. 13.

3

The Social Dynamics of Engaged Buddhism

Hope is important because it can make the present moment less difficult to bear. If we believe that tomorrow will be better, we can bear a hardship today.
– **Tech Nhat Hanh**

Introduction

No philosophy or religion would be a successful prescription to humankind unless it is practiced meticulously. Theories which do not have practical consequences remain utopian for they become oblivious over a period of time. This would have been the fate of many such great traditions like Buddhism and Vedānta. The Buddha himself engaged in disseminating his views directly to the laymen during his life time. Later on his disciples propagated the essential teachings of the Buddha. Therefore the tradition of engaged Buddhism is already present there; but it became popular in contemporary times due to the exiled Vietnamese Zen Buddhist Tech Nhat Hanh. He is a poet, teacher, author and peace activist. His motive is to apply the philosophy of Buddhism to social level by making it more practical than mere theoretical exercise. This is akin to the method followed by the great practical Vedāntins like Vivekananda and Ramatirtha who introduced the ideals of Vedānta to ordinary folk. The survival of any philosophy depends upon its social implications. In order to achieve his goal Tech Nhat Hanh combined the teaching of Mahāyāna Buddhism with the methods of Theravāda Buddhism and Western psychology. According to engaged Buddhism, the results of meditation and the teachings of *dharma* must be applied to social, political, environmental, and economic situations. The Buddha's Doctrine of Dependent Origination suggests that there is a dynamic interdependence of all phenomena. One's spiritual journey is not merely an inward exercise into one's own spiritual being, but it is a journey that goes right into the heart of the world of suffering, brokenness and imperfection. An attempt is made in this essay to show the relevance of Buddhist philosophy to contemporary society and the way in which engaged Buddhism practiced it. As a matter of fact, engaged Buddhism refers to those Buddhists who are seeking ways to apply the insights from meditational practices and *dharma* to social, economic, ecological, and environmental situations for a qualitatively better society.

What is Engaged Buddhism?

The term 'socially engaged Buddhism' refers to active involvement of Buddhists in the problems of society in order to transform the society into a society of well-being of all. In other words, it promotes egalitarian spirit among the citizens of society. The volunteers of this movement seek to actualize the philosophy of Buddhism in the contemporary world. Sometimes 'engaged Buddhism' appears to be a self-contradiction for Buddhism is seen as a passive, other worldly or escapist philosophy, for one of the most distinguishing features of Buddhism is the solitary quest for enlightenment.But engaged Buddhists do not subscribe to this view and hold "that no enlightenment can be complete as long as others remain trapped in delusion" and "that genuine wisdom is manifested in compassionate action."[1] Kraft writes: "The principles and even some of the techniques of an engaged Buddhism have been latent in the tradition since the time of its founder. Qualities that were inhibited in pre-modern Asian settings, they argue, can be actualized through Buddhism' exposure to the West, where ethical sensitivity, social activism, and egalitarianism are emphasized."[2]

According to an American Zen teacher:

> A major task for Buddhism in the west, it seems to me, is to ally itself with religious and other concerned organizations to forest

> all the potential catastrophes facing the human race: nuclear holocaust, irreversible pollution of the world's environment, and the continuing large scale destruction of non-renewable resources. We also need to lend our physical and moral support to those who are fighting hunger, poverty, and oppression in the world.[3]

Some Buddhist commentators held that we cannot plunge into immediate action rather involve people of all walks of life and make the impact massive and widespread change in the level of human consciousness. Such an effort will significantly alleviate the suffering in the world. To quote the Buddhist Ayya Khema, the German Buddhist monk, in this context:

> Every thinking person be moans the fact that there is no peace between nations. Everybody wants to see peace on the globe. Obviously there isn't any. In this century there has been a war somewhere practically all the time. Every country has an enormous defence system where a lot of energy, money, and manpower is used. This defence system is turned into an attack system the minute anyone even makes the slightest unfriendly remark or seems to be moving towards an invasion of air space or territorial waters. This is rationalised and justified with, we have to defend the boarder of our country in order to protect the inhabitants.[4]

Unfortunately disarmament remained a mere lip service and prayer, but not an actuality. Disarmament has to start in everyone's heart otherwise wholesale disarmament cannot happen. Disarmament is synonymous with nonviolence. The Tiep Hien Order of Buddhism became popular in Vietnam in 1964 during the war in Vietnam. It derives its inspiration from the Zen School of Lin Chi. The expression 'Tiep' means to continue and 'Hien' means to realize. What is to be continued and realised? Non-hatred, and tolerance towards others have to be maintained, and the Noble Truths of Buddhism have to be realised internally by every individual. The members of this group were actively engaged in spreading peace by opposing war through demonstrations and by distributing pamphlets and books. They also ran social service projects to make people aware of the evil consequences of war resulting in the death of thousands of innocent people. King Aśoka realized this after the Kaḷinga war in India and became a Buddhist monk later on. Many campaigners and the supporters of this movement died during the war. Many committed self-immolation and others died of cold-blooded murder. Thus this Order is almost wiped out in Asia. Many migrated to the west and propagated the ideology of their order to the westerners. The following are the fourteen most important precepts of this Order. They are as follows:

1. Do not be idolatrous or bound to any doctrine, theory or ideology including the Buddhist ones. All systems of thought are only guiding principles but are not absolute truth. There is no significance attached to idol worship and do not blindly adhere to any doctrine.

This precept reminds us not to be dogmatic and superstitious by following any ideology. All doctrines are only paths to reach the absolute. They are mere prescriptions, but not sacrosanct to blindly adhere. This is typically the view of Nāgārjuna, the dialectician of Mādhyamika.

2. Do not ever think that the knowledge we possess is absolute or changeless. Learn and practice non-attachment from the views in order to be open to receive others' viewpoints. Truth is found in life but not in conceptual knowledge. Knowledge is only relative and ever-changing. We should not get ourselves attached any particular view without welcoming the views of the others.

This precept reminds us that whatever we know is only relative, and do not ever think that the views of others are not worthy of consideration. There is no knowledge which is permanent. Knowledge is porous. It may come from many directions.

3. Do not force others, including children, by any means whatsoever, to adopt your views through threats, money, authority propaganda or even education. However, through compassionate dialogue help others renounce fanaticism, and narrow-mindedness. People are independent therefore we have no right to impose our views on others even if they are our near and dear. It is only through mutual interaction one can make others free from their narrow-mindedness.

This precept reminds us not to force one's views on others. The independence of others must be respected. But one can convince others through a proper dialogue, if one thinks that others are treading a wrong path.

4. Do not lose contact with suffering by closing your eyes. Do not lose the awareness of suffering around you. Try to be with those who are suffering. Just by ignoring suffering it does not disappear but face it bravely and aware of it.

This precept reminds us not to ignore suffering around us. Today it is the suffering for others and tomorrow it may be for me. Therefore, trace the root cause of suffering. By eradicating it all of us are saved from it. This precept inculcates a sense of altruism into everyone. It is the collective responsibility of all of us to fight suffering.

5. Do not accumulate wealth when millions are hungry. Do not take as the aim of your life, fame, profit, wealth or sensuous pleasure. Live simply and share time, energy, materials and natural resources with others. Try to be more humanitarian and be compassionate to others by allowing others to share your physical and mental assets.

This precept reminds us that there are others apart from you. Therefore, one needs to cultivate the sense of sharing with others the riches, fame and sensuous pleasures.

6. Do not maintain anger or hatred. When anger and hatred arise practice meditation to calm down your mind. Learn to look at others with the eyes of compassion. Anger overwhelms reason; therefore try to control your anger to resort to a meaningful action. Hatred destroys one's own personal relations with others.

This precept reminds us that anger and hatred lead to self-destruction. To control anger and hatred one needs to practice meditation for maintaining social harmony.

7. Do not lose yourself in dispersion and in your surroundings. Learn to practice breathing to regain the composure of your body and mind. One has to breathe in such a way in order to maintain the composure of your body and mind.

This precept reminds us how one should control one's breathing in order to keep one's body and mind under one's control. This is precisely what is advocated in the Patañjali yoga.

8. Do not utter words that create discord, and disharmony in the community. Make every effort to reconcile and resolve all conflicts, however small. Never try to be a foul mouth. It is only though dialogue one can resolve one's personal equations with others.

This precept reminds us not to engage one-self in hatred by using unparliamentary language against the others whereby one loses his or her relations with the others. It is through mutual dialogue personal and social conflicts can be resolved amicably.

9. Do not say untrue things for the sake of personal interest and do not utter hose words that cause division and hatred. Do not spread the news that you do not know for certain. Do not criticise or condemn the news that you are not sure of. Just to appease an individual one should not praise or hate a person for personal gains. Similarly, one should not spread false news about others.

This precept reminds us not to engage oneself in spreading rumours and false information about others for selfish gains. When one is not sure of something one should remain silent about it.

10. Do not use the Buddhist community for personal gain or profit or transform your community into a political party. A religious community should take a clear stand against oppression and injustice. The Buddhist community is meant for social welfare but not for personal welfare of any individual.

This precept reminds us not to use the Buddhist community for political purposes. The Buddhist society stands for righteousness in order to fight all forms of oppression and injustice for the betterment of social life of the individuals

11. Do not live with a vocation that is harmful to humans and nature. Do not invest in companies that deprive others their chance to live. Try to avoid taking up any form of life for the

sake of monetary gains if it is harmful to entire society like selling narcotics, dreadful weapons, liquor and so on.

This precept reminds us not to involve in trading the weapons of mass destruction, alcohol, drugs and other dangerous things for petty monetary gains.

12. Do not kill or let others kill. Find whatever means to protect life and nature and by all means prevent a war. Try to avoid violence of all sorts in order to promote peace and harmony among the people.

This precept reminds us of the significance of nonviolence in human life. Violent thought, violent speech, and violent deeds are dangerous for social harmony. They destroy individual peace as well as social peace.

13. Possess nothing that belongs to others. Respect the property of others. But prevent others from enriching themselves from human suffering. Anything and everything that is not yours should not be aspired for.

This precept reminds us not to usurp others' property and even their rights for one's own personal growth. Such an act would contribute to human suffering.

14. Do not mistreat your body. Learn to handle it with respect. Do not look on your body only as an instrument. Preserve your vital energies (sex, breath and spirit) for the realization of the way. One has to trust one's body and mind to achieve spiritual heights. Do not be little one's own capabilities.

This precept reminds us that human body is very important. Let us not belittle it for we cannot act as moral beings without the body. In order to attain moral and spiritual heights we need our body to cooperate with us.

The above are fourteen important precepts of this order. All these precepts basically represent the central doctrines of Buddhism and they are formulated to suit the needs of modern social life.The engaged Buddhists are also influenced by the Doctrine of Dependent Origination. According to them, all our experiences are interdependent and the world in which exist is an organic whole. Every event is dependent upon some other event. One event conditions the other. Thus order and purpose is inherent in the world of experiences. To quote Christopher Titmuss in this context: "One sees again and again the way mind influences the body, the body influences the mind, the way one influences the world and the world influences one."[5]Therefore, the sense of interconnectedness among the events of the world clearly shows that our responsibility to control suffering must be collective and cannot be treated as individual and isolated. The actions of an individual towards himself should not be different from his behaviour towards the society. As moral agents we must possess the sense of responsibility towards the social good. Our concern to transform society into a harmonious one for the well-being of all must be translated into a social commitment. Otherwise one does not find any link between concern and commitment. We should not transfer our responsibility to other(s). Our social obligations are our moral obligations for we are the citizens of the same society. Just as we do not expect others to eat to satiate one's hunger, one has to discharge one's social responsibilities by oneself. There is no scope for proxy here.

Concluding Remarks

Now the question is: Did Buddhism ever outlive its spirit? Buddhism by its very nature is engaged. Socially engaged Buddhism aims at spreading the Buddhist ideals as a means to healthy social practices. Buddhist monks always lived in societies and were/are asked to live among the people. Buddhism never entertained solitary life-style. The socially engaged Buddhism flourished in India, China and Vietnam. One of the most important aspects of engaged Buddhism is that every individual contributes to the welfare of society in one way or other. No individual is treated useless. What is lacking in one individual is found in another. The participatory form of life does not encourage individuals to shirk their responsibilities. We have to perform the role assigned to us with sincerely and commitment. The very survival of Buddhism for centuries together itself is an indication to the people of the world that its fundamental tenets are acceptable to the people of the world.

Notes

1. Kenneth Kraft, "Engaged Buddhism' in Arnold Kotler (ed.), *Engaged Buddhist Reader*, Berkeley: Parallax Press, 1996, p. 65.
2. *Ibid.*
3. Roshi Kapleau, "Orientalism, Ideology, and Engagement" in Harry Oldmeadow(ed.) *Journeys East:20th Century Western Encounters with Eastern Religious Traditions,* World Wisdom Inc., 2004, p. 378.
4. Ayya Khema, *Being Nobody, Going Nowhere: The Foundation of Buddhist Thought,* USA: Wisdom Publications, 1987, p. 58.
5. Christopher Titmuss, "Interactivity: Sitting for Peace and Standing for Parliament' in F. Eppsteiner (ed.), *The Path of Compassion: Writings on Socially Engaged Buddhism,* Berkeley: Parallax Press, 1985, p. 187.

4

Pūrva-Mīmāṁsā on Space and Time

Introduction

There have been many views about space and time in the history of philosophy. Both scientists and philosophers showed keen interest in defining these concepts. Thus the problem of space and time has become one of the most important problems. Indian philosophers, like their western counterparts, entered into hair splitting exercise of analyzing the concepts of space and time. The following questions often confront us while dealing with these notions. They are:

1. Are space and time substances?
2. Are space and time finite or infinite?
3. Are space and time subjective or objective?
4. Are space and time real or unreal?
5. Are space and time one or many? Are space and time perceptible or imperceptible? It is not all that easy to provide any outright answer to any one of these questions, for they lead us to scrupulous inquiry into the metaphysics of various kinds.

Any interpretation of space and time as concepts depends upon one's commitment to certain kind of metaphysics/ontology. If one were a realist, then his conception of space and time has to be realistic and objective. The Western philosophers, like Immanuel Kant, treated space and time as pure forms of sensible intuition; while McTaggart treated space and time as unreal. Similarly, the realistic systems of Indian philosophy, by and large, admitted the reality of space and time in spite of the subtle differences concerning the interpretation of these concepts. However, the trans-theistic systems like Advaita have not attached any significance to these concepts as their ultimate concern is to establish the trans-empirical nature of the supreme reality, namely, Brahman/Ātman, which is *anādi* or timeless. In other words, Advaita treats the processes of phenomenal reality as a passing phase of one's experiences.

So long as we lead our lives as empirical and pragmatic beings we cannot but reduce our experiences to spatio-temporal dimensions. The language that we use to express our day-to-day experiences necessarily involves an implicit reference to space and time. All our actions in this empirical world as moral agents are subjected to temporality. Thus space and time become adjuncts of our social actions, even if they are treated as real. The linguistic expressions of these actions refer to past, present and future. In short, the verbs that we use in our linguistic expressions have conjugations of past, present and future, but not nouns. Similarly, every action performed by us necessarily refers to certain spatial relations too. When action is performed, it is our curiosity to ask the questions---When did it happen? Where did it happen? In these interrogations, the terms 'when' and 'where' represent temporal and spatial relations of the event in question. Thus every action fits into a particular spatio-temporal framework of reference. Bereft of spatio-temporal relations everything appears to be hazy in this empirical world. It is admitted beyond doubt that space and time have become part and parcel of human life. An attempt is made in this essay to highlight Pūrva-Mīmāṁsā conception of space and time.

Pūrva-Mīmāṁsā View

Those who are familiar with Pūrva-Mīmāṁsā know that it is one of the most valued orthodox systems of Indian philosophy as it takes the *karmakāṇḍa* of the Vedas very seriously. Although one does not find much discussion on space and time in Pūrva-Mīmāṁsā, one has to infer that being a realistic system it cannot deny the reality of space and time. Pūrva-Mīmāṁsā developed a coherent system of activism which centers around the concept of '*dharma*'. All the injunctions of the Veda are considered to be *dharma,* hence it has to be practiced. In other words, *dharma* is identical with action (*karma*). We as empirical beings are considered as moral agents of actions performed in this empirical world. These actions are fitted into the spatio-temporal framework to identify the source, the place, and the time of every action.

Like Nyāya-Vaiśeṣika realism, Pūrva-Mīmāṁsā too admitted nine substances (*dravyas*). This number includes space and time. Apart from that, the Pūrva-Mīmāṁsā conception of time is akin to that of Nyāya-Vaiśeṣikain many respects. Therefore, prior knowledge of Nyāya-Vaiśeṣika conception of space and time is desirable to understand the view of Pūrva-Mīmāṁsā. According to them the substance is one of the categories (*padārthas*). And this "substance is something over and above the qualities."[1] Substance, according to these systems, is the substratum of qualities irrespective of their actual or potential nature, and is something that can exist independent of qualities, but qualities cannot exist independent of substance in which they inhere. They have mere subsistence but not existence. Further, Nyāya-Vaiśeṣika makes a distinction between eternal (*nitya*), and non-eternal (*anitya*) substances. For instance "Whatever depends on something else is not eternal. Compound substances (*avayavidravyas*) are dependent and transitory. Simple substances have the characteristics of eternity, independence, and ultimate individuality."[2] The elements like earth, water, light, air, *ākāśa*, time, space, soul, and *manas* are treated as substances. However, some of them are corporeal in nature and some of them are not. Out of these nine substances *ākāśa,* space and time are said to be all pervading (*vibhu*), and are imperceptible. Not only that, they are single substances with largest dimensions. They are supposed to be the receptacles of all corporeal things.[3] It is clear from the account given by Nyāya-Vaiśeṣika that substance is that in which qualities inhere. But in Western philosophy either the substance is one or two. Monists view that substance is one and has many qualities. But the philosophers like Descartes held that there are two substances, namely, mind and body having thinking and extension as their attributes respectively.

In the Indian context the number is not fixed at one or two as seen in the case of Nyāya-Vaiśeṣika. However, the qualities and actions do not have independent existence from substance(s). Also, Vaiśeṣika system advances certain conditions for any substance to be an object of perception. They are as follows:[4]

1. A substance must be big in the sense that it must possess molecular dimension (*mahatva*).
2. A substance must have some colour or form (*rūpa*)

If these conditions are applied to substance, then earth, water, and fire alone are considered to be the objects of perception. Since all others substances are imperceptible, their existence is only inferred. For instance, for Nyāya-Vaiśeşika, time as a substance is inferred from the notions of past, present, and future. Anything that is generated in this empirical world is generated in time. Similarly, space as a substance is inferred from the notions of near and far. Not only that, time and space as substances are infinite in their dimensions as substances. Nothing infinite, according to Nyāya-Vaiśeşika, is divisible and destroyed. Therefore, time and space are eternal (*nitya*). If time and space are indivisible, then how can anyone ascribe characteristics such as past, present, and future to time; and east, west, south and north to space? These divisions of time and directions of space are only conventional and artificial. They are grounds for our cognitions such as nearness and remoteness. Time and space are all pervasive. This is the view of Nyāya-Vaiśeşika.

Proceeding from the above view, it is said that the position of Pūrva Mīmāṁsā on space and time cannot be completely different from that of Nyāya-Vaiśeşika account. Mīmāṁsā is a combination of pluralism and realism. Like Nyāya-Vaiśeşika, Mīmāṁsā too accepts all the nine substances. However, Kumārila Bhaṭṭa, one of the chief exponents of *karma* Mīmāṁsā, adds two more to the list of substances of Nyāya-Vaiśeşika. They are darkness and sound. Bust his disciple, Prabhākara, rejects them. Well, we are not concerned with these two substances at present. Our main concern is to understand the nature of space and time as substances. However, both Kumārila and Prabhākara have accepted them as substances.[5]

Kumārila argues that time and space are perceptible. This goes against the view of Nyāya-Vaiśeşika. According to him, every perceptual experience, irrespective of its perceptual source, refers to time. Similar argument can be advanced to show that even space is perceptible. Both time and space cannot be apprehended directly. But only with reference to some objects. This is the reason why a Mīmāṁsāka treats time and space as two adjuncts of any action. Since action is performed by an individual as a moral agent, time and space become two important modes of every action. Even material objects involve in various processes. But these processes cannot be the processes apart from the observer.[6]

Further, the Mīmāṁsākas argue that Nayyāyikas –Vaiśeṣikas held the view that the existence of time and space as substances is inferred from the sense of events like slowness, quickness, and the sense of directions like east, west, south and north respectively. Since time and space have infinite dimensions, they cannot be perceived. Apart from that, they are devoid of colour, which is visually apprehended. Against these arguments of Nyāya-Vaiśeṣika, Pūrva-Mīmāṁsā holds that it is no argument to put forward that time and space are not amenable to perceptual experience because they lack sensible colour (*udbhūtarūpa*). It is in a way a fallacy of generalizing a rule (hasty generalization) which is found to be true in specific cases. As a matter of fact, it is an accident that some objects of perception possess colours and others do not. For example, what is the colour of water? It does not have any colour, yet we perceive it as a substance. Hence the argument against the perceptible nature of time and space is illogical. Further the quality of colour, though devoid of colour, is visually perceived. Atoms are infra sensible in spite of the colour present in them.[7] Thus the perception of time in spite of its colournessness is a fact of experience. Therefore, it cannot be invalidated by any law.

In fact, Kant in his *Critique of Pure Reason* advances similar argument like Pūrva-Mīmāṁsā. The notions of space and time cannot be arrived at by any process of ratiocination. According to Kant, both space and time are pure forms of intuition. They are neither concepts nor percepts. They are necessary elements in all our day-to-day experiences. But Pūrva-Mīmāṁsā differs from Kant, as a realist school, by holding the view that time and space have objective existence. For Kant, space and time are *a priori.* On the contrary, both time and space are substances having real existence for Pūrva-Mīmāṁsā. Apart from that, Kant's position on space and time results in some inconsistencies. One can ask: How is it possible for pure forms of intuition to have anything to do with sense-experience? If there is any relation between the forms of intuition and sense-experience, how is this relation related to the forms of intuition one side and the sense-experience on the other? Kant cannot explain this point. His attempt was a failure. Instead Kant could have accommodated space and time in the appearance(*śvarūpa*) of phenomenon.[8]

Concluding Remarks

One can notice that there are certain inconsistencies in the position taken by Pūrva-Mīmāṁsā. It claims that time and space are substances. At the same time it treats them as relations too for they connect objects of the empirical world. Now the question arises: How can substances be turned into relations? A Mīmāṁsāka may reply that time and space are included in the appearance of every object, since every object appears to be temporal as well as spatial. Even if this fact is conceded, yet a Mīmāṁsāka cannot explain how this appearance is treated as a relation. When anyone perceives an object at the most what he perceives is its spatiality or extension, but not its temporality. Then how can Mīmāṁsākas account for time as a perceptual relation? Not only that, if space and time are treated as substances, then they cannot be related to objects for which they are attributes to be related to any content.

Another point at issue is that if space and time are infinite in their extension, then each one as a substance limits the other. Further, as infinite substances they cannot be fit into our visual field. Therefore, they cannot be perceived. If space and time are substances with all pervading nature, then they cannot change. Well, such a view may go well with space but not with time as time is unidimensional in that it has characteristics of past, present and future. These characteristics enable us to divide time into hours, days, weeks, and years. Therefore, all pervading nature of time and its characteristics in terms of change contradict each other. If the divisions of time are only conventional, then our conception of time may lead to certain absurdities. For example, one may say that Socrates and Gandhi are contemporaries, "for changeless time is contemporaneous or the eternally present."[9] In that sense time is not different from space. In order to show that Socrates lived much before Gandhi, we have to accept the changing nature of time, and its divisions of past, present, and future as real. Hence, Pūrva-Mīmāṁsā is wrong in holding the view that time is one and eternal. If time is eternal, then it is as good as living in timelessness.

Then another misconception of Mīmāṁsākas is that for any object to be real is to be perceived. It need not be the case always. To say that some object is real is to say that it has objective significance. Both space and time have objective significance. Every object exists within space and time. Therefore, space and time are external to things. In fact, they relate objects of the world, but not as relations. The contiguous and co-existence of objects, and their existence in various time intervals are possible due to space and time. In this sense it is unimaginable to think of them as substances having independent existence. The dynamic nature of reality would not be grasped without space and time, and they are not indifferent to objects existing in this world. Not only that, both space and time have objective significance to one who experiences various processes of the empirical world. Being adjuncts of every human action, space and time become naturally objective.

Another defect of Mīmāṁsākas is that they hold the view that space is primarily the ground for idea of nearness and distantness, and secondarily divided into directions such as east, west, etc. But, is the primary definition of space primary? The supposed characteristics of space, namely, near and far are only relative in their nature. What is nearer to someone may be far off to another. How can such characteristics be treated as primary? When the Mīmāṁsākas say that time and space are infinite in their extension, in order to perceive them one must go beyond them. This is a self-contradiction in terms.

The above inconsistencies in the thesis of Pūrva-Mīmāṁsā clearly vindicate that space and time cannot be treated as substances. They are only relations which connect objects and processes in which objects of the world are involved. They have objective existence since they are part and parcel of human experiences. In this sense alone they are treated as real. Here in this context 'real' is used in the sense of 'objective'. Space makes an act of locating objects possible, whereas time helps us in distinguishing the events of the past from those of present and future. Everything that takes place in this phenomenal world is fitted into spatio-temporal framework.

When we see the classification of substances made by Jainism, we come across that time and space are treated as non-material and inanimate substances.Thus they are non-extended substances. Further time is divided into real time (*pāramārthika*) and conventional time (*vyāvahārika*). This classification of time of Jainism sounds logical, but the question arises: How is conventional time related to real time? One does not find any clue in the philosophy of Jainism. We as empirical individuals are not concerned with real time, but are concerned with conventional one. The real time, according to Jainism, is continuous duration and there are no divisions in it. We can only infer that all changes are due to the continuous duration of real time, for it is imperceptible. It is as good as timelessness. How does anyone know that we are under constant duration? In other words, one cannot notice any changes under continuous duration. All changes are subjected to this continuous duration of real time. Interestingly, Jainism claims that there are infinite number of particles of time and each of which is indivisible. These particles of time cannot be divided into timeless points. The apparent contradiction in Jaina theory of time is that real time is indivisible, yet it consists of particles of time. Is real time made up of particles of time? Then it loses its continuity for there must be something to connect one particle with the other for they are discrete and unconnected. Further Jainism maintains that real time being non-extended, it does not occupy space. If time is made up of particles of time, then each of that particle must be an extended one. If particles of time are non-extended then they are metaphysical entities, and the real time is also made up of these metaphysical entities. Coming to conventional time, it is divided into years, seasons, months, weeks, days, and so on.[10]

Space is also treated as a substance by Jainism. It is a receptacle for all the objects of extension. Space is one, infinite, indivisible, and eternal. But it is not the cause of objects. Prior to the existence of objects both space and time must be there. It is an indispensable condition. Like time, space too cannot be perceived but can only be inferred. Like time, space too is divided by Jainism into world-space (*lokākāśa*) and non-world-space (*alokākāśa*). The empirical objects occupy this world-space and the non-world-space is that which transcends the world–space. To use Kantian distinction here, Jainism admits world-space (phenomenal realm) and the non-world-space (noumenal realm).

But both are one and continuous. It implies that there is unoccupied space beyond the world-space.

Like Pūrva-Mīmāṁsā, Jainism too did not advance a satisfactory thesis concerning space and time. If time is considered to be a continuous duration, then within that the duration of life span cannot be measured. In order to measure time it has to be an extended substance. Then real time is non-extended and the conventional one is extended. Here is an apparent contradiction. If both forms of time are one and same, then time is either extended or non-extended. It cannot be both. If the definition of Jainism concerning time is taken into consideration, then time is that which measures one's growth from childhood to the end of one's span of life. Then time is extended unlike space. Jainism answers this objection by holding the view that "what we call time, space, rest, and movement are not what we observe with our senses, but what make these phenomena possible."[11] Only when we make units of space and time, these units as a series of static pictures are observable. As rightly held by P.T. Raju: "If every picture is static, how can movement come out of them by simply attaching them to one another? So movement, in the sense of what makes observable movement possible, we have to admit, is not observable. Similarly, time, space and rest in the sense of the agencies which make the observable time, space, and rest possible, cannot be observed. Then, where are they, as the roots of our experiences, located?"[12] This is an important observation. What is static cannot explain the dynamic movement of time. And it is not all that easy for Jainism to answer this question.

It is clear that Pūrva-Mīmāṁsā, like Jainism, recognized both absolute and relative time forms of space, and time. However, the relative space, and relative are not different from absolute space, and absolute time. The perceptible world of objects being relative, both space and time that we experience as adjuncts of objects are also relative. Even our sources of knowledge (*pramāṇas*) are the aids with the help of which we obtain the knowledge of empirical world. Our finite minds are incapable of apprehending anything infinite, but it is through the method of presupposition (*arthāpatti*) we come to know about the existence of the infinite space, and the infinite time. Yet the problem is not completely resolved, for we believe in the existence of more than one infinite, namely, space and time.

Notes

1. S. Radhakrishnan, *Indian Philosophy*, Delhi: Motilal Banarsidass, Vol.II, 1989, p. 188.
2. *Ibid.*
3. *Ibid.,* p. 189.
4. P.T. Raju, *Structural Depths of Indian Thought*, New Delhi: South Asian Publishers, 1985, p. 255.
5. M. Hiriyanna, *Outlines of Indian Philosophy*, New Delhi: Blackie & Son (India LTD), 1979, p. 324.
6. C.D. Sharma, A *Critical Survey of Indian Philosophy*, Delhi: Motilal Banarsidass, 1979, p. 233.
7. Jayanta Bhatta, *Nyāyamañjari* (trans. & ed.), Varanasi: Kashi Sanskrit Series, 1936, p. 124.
8. P.T. Raju, *Structural Depths of Indian Thought*, 1985, p. 239.
9. *Ibid.,* p. 290.
10. *Ibid.,* p. 122.
11. *Ibid.,* p. 130.
12. *Ibid.*

5

Philosophical and Spiritual Dimensions of Yoga

Introduction

It is believed that the practice of *yoga* for the sake of self-realization is much older than the Vedas. It is a technique or a method to control body and mind to achieve self-perfection. It appears that there are evidences to show the practice of yoga during Mohenjo-daro civilization. But Yoga as expounded by Patañjali is treated as an allied system of Sāṅkhya by the classical Indian tradition. The term *'yoga'* is derived from the Sanskrit root '*yuj*', which literally means 'union'. It is a union of individual soul with the spiritual soul.[1] It also means to join' or to yoke. As a matter of fact, it is a method that joins the finite spirit with the infinite or supreme Spirit. In other words, *yoga* is self-realization in its widest sense of the term.[2] This method consists of the techniques or practices leading to the union or self-realization (*viveka-jñāna*). Even if one does not believe in the spiritual knowledge, one may practice *yoga* to keep one's mind and body healthy and agile.

The famous *Yogasūtras,* the aphorisms of Yoga, were composed by the sage Patañjali around 4th century BC. But, it was Vyāsa who wrote a commentary on Patañjali's *Yogasūtras* around 4th century AD. Patañjali Yoga is also popularly known as *Raja Yoga. Yogasūtras* are divided into four parts, namely, *Samādhipāda, Sādhanapāda*,

Vibhūtipāda, and *Kaivalyapāda.* The first part deals with the nature and aim of concentration, the second with the means to realize this end, the third with the supra-normal powers that one can acquire through yoga, and the fourth with the nature of liberation and the reality of the supreme transcendental Self.[3] Being an allied system of Sāṅkhya, Yoga accepts the metaphysical and epistemological framework of the former.

Epistemology

Like Sāṅkhya, Yoga too admits three valid sources of knowledge, namely, perception *(pratyakṣa*), inference (*anumāna*), and verbal testimony(*śabda*). Patañjali recasts the Sāṅkhya position on cognition. It is held by Sāṅkhya that cognition is a transformation and modification of impersonal Reason (*buddhi*, Mahat). But in reality, according to Yoga, everything undergoes modification, including the objects of the physical world. These modifications are classified into five functions (*vṛttis).* They are: the valid sources of knowledge (*pramāṇas*), wrong or false knowledge (*viparyaya),* empty concepts (*vikalpas*), sleep (*nidrā*), and memory (*smṛti*). Sleep is a kind of experience wherein there is an experience of mere absence. The valid sources of knowledge mentioned above represent the right cognition. It must be noted here that Reason (Mahat) is not to be understood as an ordinary reasoning process rather it is the all-pervading metaphysical principle out of which everything originates. It is also the source of ego.

The essential characteristic of this Reason is 'am-ness' (*asmitā*) or 'I am'(*ahamasmi*). The 'I' in this context cannot be equated with ego but something higher than it. It is impersonal, yet it experiences itself as 'am'. In other words, to say that the empirical world is rational is to say that it is the assertion of an impersonal Reason. The impersonal Reason operates through the ego in spite of the fact that the former transcends the latter. The ego accepts the assertions of the impersonal Reason as its assertions and identifies itself with the impersonal Reason. The five functions listed above are the modifications of the impersonal Reason that are associated with the ego.[5] Further it is observed that even the empty concepts are also modifications of impersonal Reason. The cognition through an empty concept is defined as the cognition that follows upon a word which does not correspond to anything in objective reality.[6] According to Yoga, *ātman* by itself is considered to be consciousness. However, we tend to speak of consciousness of ātman as if consciousness is as an attribute of ātman forgetting the fact that ātman is consciousness. All these aberrations occur due to the misuse of language. In this sense *vikalpa* means the ideational, the conceptual, the imaginary, the fanciful, or what is mentally created. Mind has the capacity to create such concepts which do not signify anything in objective reality. Patańjali warns of such *vikalpas*.

By sleep Yoga means deep sleep, which is a dreamless state. It is also treated as a modification of impersonal Reason (Mahat). As such it involves consciousness but not unconscious. It cannot be regarded as the consciousness of absence (nothingness) rather it is treated as the presence of consciousness even if all other functions are absent. Even in sleep there is consciousness for otherwise when a person wakes up he or she cannot say "I slept well". Illusion (*viparyaya*) is another modification of mind. Unlike Sāṅkhya, Yoga treats it as false knowledge. Such a form of knowledge results from the perception of a non-existent form (*atadrūpapratiṣṭham*).[7] The object perceived in illusion does not exist, but for Sāṅkhya it exists for it is only the modification (*pariṇāma*) of the real object. Thus it is both existent and non-existent. According to Yoga, illusion is caused by five impurities. They are: ignorance (*avidyā*), false identification of oneself with objective world or egoism (*asmitā*), attachment (*rāga*), hate (*dveṣa*) and self-attachment (*abhiniveśa*), which is accompanied by the anxiety of death.[8]

Yoga also recognises five levels of mental life (*cittabhūmi*). These levels are caused by the predominance of different *guṇas*.Restlessness or *kṣipta* is caused by the excess of rajas. This is supposed to be the lowest mental level. The next level is torpid or *mudha*. The mind has more of *tamas* which makes it ignorant, dull and sleepy. The next higher stage is called distracted (*vikṣipta*). Here in this stage although *sattva* is a dominating *guṇa*, yet rajas too asserts itself at times. Therefore, the mind gets distracted. The next higher stage is called concentration (*ekāgra*). Here in this stage the mind is completely dominated by *sattva*. The mind can concentrate on the object of its choice without any hindrance. The fifth and the highest stage is called restricted (*nirudha*). The mental modifications in this stage are completely arrested though their latent impressions remain. These stages proceed in an ascending order. The first three stages are not conducive for yogic practices. The last two alone are the proper stages for taking up yogic life.[9]

Metaphysics

Although Yoga admits the metaphysical foundations of Sāṅkhya, yet Patañjali adds up something more in the following way. First of all, he goes deeper into the analysis of the nature of transformation. Secondly, he admits the existence of God unlike Sāṅkhya. Thirdly, he attempts to show the relation between the impersonal Reason and moral action.

According to Sāṅkhya, everything is under constant transformation (*pariṇāma*). There is nothing which does not undergo transformation. This view of Sāṅkhya is akin to Buddhist doctrine of momentariness. In other words, it amounts to saying that there is nothing permanent or stable substance to which change belongs to. But both Sāṅkhya and Yoga admit the existence of Prakṛti, the primordial, eternal substance to which all change belongs to. The change is only the modification of Prakṛti's attributes only. Sāṅkhya does not discuss this relation between substance (*dharmī*) and its attributes (*dharmas*) at all. Patañjali discusses this relation between substance and its attributes (qualities) in detail. If there is persisting change in everything at every moment, then how do we distinguish between substance and its attributes (qualities)? Patañjali makes an attempt to show how we can distinguish substance, attributes (qualities) and their changes within this continual change.

There is nothing special about the view that every transformation is a modification. For example, water transforms into ice at a particular temperature. Such a modification has three aspects within it. They are: modification of substance, modification of quality, and modification of the mode of quality. In the example given above, water modifies into ice. The former is in liquid form and the latter is hard. What we observe here is the modification of one quality into another (*dharmapariṇāma*). The substance remains the same. The change occurs within the same substance. This passage of change takes place through three moments, past, present and future. Therefore, there occurs change in the modes of existence of substance. Further, it is also stated by Patañjali that each state of change has three moments-strong, weak and submerged.

When the change is clearly observed it is strong and slowly becomes weak when it is going to be taken over by the next state. When it is completely overwhelmed then it submerges into the next state.[10] Since these three stages are continuously overlapping with each other there exists no interval of nothingness *(sūnyata)*. What is interesting to note here is that in all these three stages the substance remains the same. We can only observe the modifications of substance but not substance as it is too subtle.[11]

From the above analysis of change we find that substance is the individual (*vyakti*). Its accompanying qualities alone change but substance remains the same. Substance possesses elements of stability in the object observed. As Raju puts it: "Change is not within time; on the other hand time is constituted by, and is none other than the three moments of the changing quality."[12] Similarly, space is only an extended property of substances. It has no reality of its own. Both time and space are only the forms of ether (*akāśa*), which is the ground for the possibility of change of objects and their extendedness. Time and space, according to Yoga, are only the aspects of the transformation of objects. Substance is the generator of qualities, including time and space. Time is only the name given to the three moments of change of qualities. The individuality of substance can be explained in the following manner. Substance exists whereas qualities subsist in substance. In other words, substance for its existence is not dependent on qualities, but qualities need substance for their subsistence. This is the contribution of Patañjali to the concept of substance. He agrees with Sāṅkhya that there is change in everything.

God

Accepting the reality of God is another salient feature of Yoga. Patañjali holds that stopping of the five functions of Reason is the prime objective of Yoga. It is a difficult task for the nature of Reason is such that it is always active. When all its functions are stopped it goes to sleep, which is also its function. In that case it must be allowed to function and that would be to meditate on God in order to attain salvation.[13] God being omniscient there is no knowledge greater than His. God is not touched by the five impurities- ignorance, sense of ego, desire, hate, and fear of death. Also, he is not touched by the results of ethical actions and the potencies left by ethical actions (*karmāśayas*). God is Puruṣa, but of a special kind (*puruṣaviśeṣa*).[14] He is not bound by time and is a teacher of all gods. Meditation of God involves repeating his name and thinking of its meaning. Through meditation mind becomes totally inward and all obstacles to meditation such as disease, lethargy, doubt, in attention, heaviness of body and mind attachment to objects, error, inexplicable failure to obtain trance, and unsteadiness to mind are overcome.[15]

Patañjali does not offer any proof(s) for the existence of God unlike Western theologians. He only gave some descriptions about God and the advantages of meditating on him. But the commentators like Vijñānabhikṣu forced some arguments into these descriptions of Patañjali. It is argued by the former that scriptures are absolutely authentic and they say about God's existence. Therefore, God exists. Another argument is that men possess different degrees of knowledge. There must be some upper and lower limit. The upper limit of knowledge is possessed by God and there is no knowledge greater than that.

Reason and Action

How do moral actions effect the change of our personality in terms of character? These changes would further effect the dynamic forces that are responsible for our future births. Yoga accepts the doctrine of *karma* and reincarnation. The moral actions leave their potencies (*samskāras*) in the impersonal Reason. These potencies later on become the modifications of the creative energy of Reason (*buddhi, citta*). Thus Reason of every individual is modified in a different way according to the actions performed by the individual. The world comes out of such a modified Reason. In other words, Reason is the ultimate ontological principle for this school. Our bodies are also the evolutes of Reason. Hence they are not the agents of enjoyment, but only the instruments of Reason. The ultimate enjoyer is the "I" as the ego.

Reason, according to Yoga, has two aspects. One aspect of it creates the world that is shared by all of us. The common world is the given world. The other aspect of Reason makes the world different to each individual in terms of its enjoyment. What produces pleasure in one individual may produce pain or agony in another. These differences are due to the actions performed by the individuals as moral agents.

The potencies of moral actions accumulate together and constitute the reservoir of potencies. This reservoir of potencies becomes one of the afflictions (*kleśas*) of Reason, which creates a distorted world of colourful objects. This part of Reason is known as the Reason of action-potencies. These potencies do not manifest all at a time. Some of them are known in this present birth and some in future births.[16]The results produced by these potencies manifest in the form of birth, duration of life and nature of enjoyments. These are the three fountains on which human life is built up. It is left to the individual's freedom to perform new actions to cancel them or to improve upon them or not to perform any action. These potencies produce their effects insofar as the original ignorance between the Prakṛti and Puruṣa continues. Through the practice of yoga the discrimination dawns on the individual and the ignorance is dispelled. But among those potencies that have started afresh in the present life alone bear the fruit and the others get dried up to become like dead seeds. Thus the doctrine of *karma* becomes teleological in Yoga. Without any reference to God, Yoga explains the cessation of these potencies through the practice of yoga.

The Techniques of Yoga

The ultimate aim of Yoga, like any other orthodox Indian philosophical system, is to attain liberation, which is known as *samādhi.* How does one attain it? Before we discuss the methods of attaining *samādhi,* it is necessary to explain what *samādhi* means. The English translations of the word 'sa*mādhi'* are highly misleading. The word is translated as trance, ecstasy, rapture, concentration and so on. None of these translations is accurate. To be in the state of trance means to be in the state of morbidity. Ecstasy means an exalted feeling, rapture is a kind of being carried away by means of attraction, and concentration is a mental feeling of fixing one's mind on an object of one's choice. But *samādhi* cannot be equated with any one of these psychological states or processes. Etymologically the word means settling down of Reason on something.[17] It implies peace and steadiness. In other words, it is the settling of Reason in itself.

The practice of yoga is to stop or damn the functions of Reason. When these functions are stopped Reason becomes completely transparent as it purges out disturbances, agitations, and all other outgoing activities. Even sleep, one of the functions of Reason, has to be stopped. The Reason stays in itself and is conscious. Its consciousness is the reflection of the Puruṣa. There is nothing objective to know. Such a state is technically called *samādhi.* To attain it is the ultimate goal of Yoga.

Modern psychologists are of the view that most of the conscious processes and their structures are hidden from us in the depth of the subconscious and the unconscious. Even the philosophers of Yoga such as Patańjali realised it long before Freud or Young. Most of these levels of consciousness are hidden from our awareness. For the sake of brevity and convenience let us reduce these conscious processes and their structures into attentive and non-attentive or residual modes. The attentive mode represents all those conscious processes, structures and their contents illumined by witnessing consciousness or individual reason. We are fully aware of the conscious level of our own mental life as opposed to the subconscious or unconscious levels that contain non-attentive or residual mode of consciousness. This mode of consciousness traces the impressions or potencies buried in the totality of human experience. It is much deeper and pervasive than the attentive mode. This non-attentive or residual consciousness accounts for most of our conditioning.[18] These primary forces which reside in the hidden level of consciousness make up our personality, and are responsible for creating our personal identity. These powerful forces have to be brought back from darkness to self-awareness for otherwise they keep us in perennial bondage. Once they are brought back to the mode of attentive consciousness they are gradually eliminated or put to complete rest through yogic practices.

Although physical and metal exercises help us to some extent in attaining *samādhi*, the most important starting point is the purification of one's Reason. This Reason (I-am) represents one's personal being. So long as it is driven by the residual conscious forces it cannot be pure and attain stability. It would be constantly fluctuating. Its steadiness and stability can be achieved through proper practice *(abhyāsa)* and detachment (*vairāgya*) from objects. The control over longing for something can be achieved by cultivating friendship with those who are happy without being envious, and by showing compassion towards those who are in sorrow, and by being pleasant without being jealous towards the others who are meritorious. Apart from that one must also practice self-control, non-injury, non-stealing, truthfulness, celibacy, and non-acceptance of gifts. Everyone can practice these virtues even if one does not care for liberation. It is also held that the sense of detachment would be complete in itself through *Īśvara-prānidhāna* or constant contemplation of the Supreme Being, who is free from all works and afflictions and having the appellation *Om* or *praṇava.*[19] The repetition (*smaraṇa*) of this mono syllable has its own miraculous effects. It is conducive to the knowledge of the supreme and also for the prevention of all impediments to yoga.

Coming to the steadiness of mind, only fortunate ones alone can attain it. But others who want to control their mind have to put in rigorous effort for that. One easy method is to meditate on God or one may practice measured inhaling and exhaling (*prāṇāyāma*). When inhaling and exhaling are done in an irregular manner it results in mental agitation. First of all mind has to be fixed on the measures of breath controlling its agitation is minimised. Another way is to remove all attachments from mind in order to make it steady. One can also meditate on the consciousness present in dream or deep sleep. It is not the meditation on the objects of consciousness, but on that consciousness itself. It is the concentration on its very essence that represents the ontological or impersonal Reason (Mahat). Or one can fix one's mind on the objects of one's liking. These are all only the aids to attain the steadiness of mind. Once the effort of fixing mind is complete, then it passes through five important stages(*bhūmis*). Here the mind refers to Reason which is variously known as *citta, buddhi* and Mahat, the nature of which changes at every instance. When we attempt to make Reason steady it becomes agitated and restless (*kṣipta*). When a greater force is thrust on it to fix it, it becomes torpid (*mūḍha*), a tendency to fall asleep. When we still make greater effort, it becomes distracted *(vikṣipta*). If we continue to put greater effort then it becomes concentrated (*ekāgra*) on the object of meditation. Finally, when we make a steady effort to make our mind stay on in that state it becomes restrained (*niruddha*) and all its functions stop. The last two stages are important for attaining *samādhi.*[20]

The Eight-Fold Path (*Aṣṭānga-Yoga*)

The practices prescribed so far are not all that easy to follow. Our mundane existence is the being of Prakṛti which is under constant change. In the process of meditation we are supposed to go against our very mundane nature. Therefore, Patañjali suggests eight steps or limbs (*aṅgas*) to be practiced step by step. But it should not be assumed that the earlier steps or methods are to be discarded in favour of the later ones. The steadiness of mind is absolutely necessary for practicing *aṣṭānga-yoga.* In a way both the earlier and later steps go well with each other. One cannot provide a solution to a mathematical problem without knowing the integers and their values. Similar is the case with these steps. The *astānga-yoga*, which is also known as Rāja-yoga, includes self-control (*yama*), regulation of life by certain rules (*niyama*), bodily postures (*āśanas*), breath-control (*prāṇayāma*), withdrawal of senses from the external objects (*pratyāhāra),* fixing the mind on an object (*dhāraṇa*), meditation (*dhyāna*), and *samādhi.* Let us examine them in detail.

Self-control (*yama*)

It is of five types. They are: non-injury, truthfulness, non-stealing, celibacy, and non-acceptance of gifts. In other words, one should not accept anything that is an instrument of pleasure.

Rules for Regulating Life (*niyama*)

These rules include the purification of body, both externally and internally. This purification starts with cleaning of body through washing, and by taking clean and pure food. Internally mind has to be cleansed by practicing friendship, kindness towards the others, cheerfulness, and indifference to the voices of others. Apart from these, contentment, penance by practicing austerities, regular study of sacred books and meditation on God are recommended.

Bodily Postures (*āśanas*)

Normally people think that practicing yoga means only to practice some prescribed *āśanas* by the guru. They are only part of the limbs of yoga but do not represent yoga in its entirety. The purpose of these bodily postures is to keep our body under our control. These postures keep our body steady during meditation so that no discomfort may distract our mind from concentration. Of course, it is not denied that some of the postures help body to keep its agility. A healthy body is a prerequisite for meditative practices. There are many postures prescribed in the Rāja-yoga. These postures are chosen by the practitioners of yoga to suit their requirement.

Breath-control (*prāṇayāma*)

Through this process we are supposed to regulate our inhaling and exhaling. This act is of several kinds. By practicing breath-control one can achieve control over one's involuntary functions too. Irregular breathing leads to mental agitations and lack of concentration. To arrest mental agitations breath-control is practiced. It is also believed by Sāṅkhya-Yoga that the life-principle (*prāṇa*) functions involuntarily in our bodies, and is the function of inner sense. This life-principle operates through breathing. Human body operates though many involuntary functions such as muscular and nervous activities, the assimilation of food into the body. Through breath-control we can also regulate our involuntary activities too. Apart from inhaling and exhaling, yoga also recognised the acts of retention of inhaled air in our lungs and emptying the lungs for sometime without immediately inhaling after exhaling. All these four activities have to be regulated in terms of proper time intervals. Through practice one can also stop the act of inhaling for a longer period without losing life, thus one can gain control over life-principle. But, the higher levels of breath control are not usually recommended for ordinary practitioners.

Sense-withdrawal (*pratyāhāra*)

This is another important and difficult task for a yoga practitioner. He/she has to withdraw his/her senses from external objects which cause desires in us. One has turn one's senses inward though rigorous practice in order to make senses unite with their sources. It is not destruction of senses at all. When the senses are withdrawn the external objects to which senses are attracted are also withdrawn. The senses become one with Reason. In other words, the senses are completely conquered by the practitioner of yoga.

Concentration (*dhāraṇa*)

It is an important step towards meditation. Generally concentration makes us fixing our inner sense on a desired object. It is the activity of centring our mind. The object on which the mind concentrates may be an external object, an idol, or an image of God, or any part of one's own body. Normally it is easy to concentrate on an external object or an image of God.

Meditation (*dhyāna)*

It is a steady and unbroken continuity of concentration. In this state of Reason the object on which mind concentrates becomes continuous like a flow like oil in which the drops cannot be distinguished from one another.

Samādhi

One does not find an English equivalent to this word. In the stage of meditation Reason can distinguish between the object and cognition and also knows itself as knowing object. But in the stage of *samādh*i Reason is completely absorbed in the object that the object alone stands. In this state there is no sense, no awareness, or sense of being aware of the object. The inner structure of the object reveals itself completely whether it is a physical object or one's own mind with its layers of the Unconscious, or somebody else's mind.

As described above the last three limbs or states of yoga or inner (*antaraṅga*) and the first five are external (*bahiraṅga*). Further *samādhi* is classified into two kinds. They are: *samprajṅāta* and *asamprajṅāta*. In the former the consciousness of the object of meditation persists, and in the latter it is transcended.[21] In the state of *samprajṅāta-samādhi* one who practices meditation and the object of meditation are fused together, yet the object of meditation remains. This state again is classified into *savitarka, savicāra, sąnanda,* and *sāsmita.* In the *savitarka* state the mind concentrates on the gross object of meditation like tip of one's nose, or the mid-point of the eyebrows or the image of god. In the *savacāra* state the mind concentrates on a subtler object of meditation like the *tanmātrās.*In the *sānanda* state mind concentrates on a still subtler object of meditation that produces joy. In the state of *sāsmita* the mind concentrates on the ego substance with which the self is generally identified. Here the individuality persists and the individual will have conscious ecstasy. On the contrary, in the state of *asamprajñāta-samādhi* the meditator and the object of meditation are completely fused together. No new mental modifications arise in this state. They are completely put down (*niruddha*), although their latent impressions may continue. This is the highest state of yoga which is difficult to attain. Such an experience cannot be described too. After attaining this state, the body breaks down and the person in question attains liberation.

Concluding Remarks

One of the noticeable contributions of Patañjali is his notion of *samādhi*. It has two dimensions, namely, phenomenological and existential. The ego is entangled with the objects of the phenomenal world. The phenomenological consciousness covers all empirical aspects of the world including one's own existence. But this phenomenological consciousness is only the intentional aspect of the existential consciousness. The former cannot exist without the later. The real phenomenological and existential analysis of self starts from the ideal of self-analysis. Through this analysis one can reach the core of the self (*ātman*). In fact, the different stages of *samādhi* represent different states of *ātman.*A perfect understanding of our psycho-physical being is necessary before we undergo spiritual realization. As emphasized by the Buddha, first of all, we have to develop right views or true views (*samyak-darśana*) about our own psycho-physical being. Therefore, the dictum 'know thyself' becomes very important. Patañjali virtually analysed the various levels of self-consciousness that ultimately lead us to the inner core of the self (*ātman*).

One has to carefully observe that *samādhi* for Patañjali is not merely concentrating on an object of one's desire or self-hypnotic state. Its real essence is to centrifuge the diversified energies of our own being. In one form of *samādhi* there is a known in the form of an object, and in another form there is no object to be known. The former possess the consciousness of the object, and in the latter there is no consciousness of an object. The former operates at the empirical level through *antahkaraṇa,* the subtle elements, and the gross elements. At this level of concentration there appear only two factors, namely, mind and 'am-ness' (*asmitā*). The ego (*aham*) which normally appropriates the experiences of objects as mine is transcended as 'am-ness'.

Although it exists as first person, but it is bereft of ego. Transcendence of ego is one of the fundamental features of Pantañjali's philosophy. When someone is completely absorbed in his/her thought one forgets himself/herself as there remain only thoughts. This is the pure state of 'am-ness'. The thoughts are in one's consciousness, in one's awareness, but ego is not present there. This pure thinking without the 'I' is possible because there exists pure 'I-am or am-ness'. Therefore, it is through the phenomenological reduction of ego one can attain the status of 'am-ness'.

The ultimate aim of a person who resorts to yogic practices is to attain liberation, which is a state of freedom from the entanglement of Prakṛti. One who gets entangled with the various forms of Prakṛti identifies with its forms and with the functions of Reason **(buddhi, Mahat),** which is its first evolute. Thus one identifies oneself with Reason, ego, mind, senses and physical body. One's liberation lies in getting disentangled with the above mentioned forms of Prakṛti. Yoga provides a way to get oneself disentangled from such a state to attain liberation. However, one can also practice Yoga for keeping one's mind and body fit enough for his/her day-to-day activities, and for maintaining self-discipline.

Notes

1. C. D. Sharma, *A Critical Survey of Indian Philosophy,* Delhi: Motilal Banarsidass, 1979 (Reprint), p. 169.
2. P.T. Raju, *Structural Depths of Indian Thought,* New Delhi: South Asia Publishers, 1985, p. 337.
3. C.D. Sharma, *A Critical Survey of Indian Philosophy,* p. 169.
4. P.T. Raju, *Structural Depths of Indian Thought*, New Delhi, South Asia Publications 1985, p. 338.
5. *Ibid.,* p, 339.
6. Patañjali's *Yogasūtras* with the Commentaries of Vyāsa, Vācasapati and Bhoja, I, 9.
7. *Ibid.,* I, 8.
8. C.D. Sharma, *A Critical Survey of Indian Philosophy,* p. 171.
9. *Ibid.*
10. P.T. Raju, *Structural Depths of Indian Thought*, pp. 340-41.
11. *Ibid.*
12. *Ibid.*

13. Patañjali's *Yogasūtras* with the Commentaries of Vyāsa, Vācasapati and Bhoja, I, 23.
14. *Ibid.*
15. *Ibid.*, p. 342.
16. Patañjali's *Yogasūtras* with the commentaries of Vyāsa, Vācasapati and Bhoja, I, 23.
17. P.T. Raju, *Structural Depths of Indian Philosophy,* p. 344.
18. John M. Koller, *Oriental Philosophies,* New York: Charles Scribner's Sons, 1970, p. 172.
19. Monier Williams, *The Indian Way*, New Delhi: Pearson Prentice Hall, 2007, pp. 110-11.
20. P.T. Raju, *Structural Depths of Indian Philosophy,* p. 345.
21. C.D. Sharma, *A Critical Survey of Indian Philosophy*, p. 173.

6

A Phenomenological Approach to I-Consciousness with Special Reference to P.T. Raju

Introduction

P.T. Raju is regarded as one of the foremost representatives of Indian philosophy in general, and Advaita in particular in the contemporary philosophical scenario. His corpus of writings on these subjects bears testimony to this fact. One of the most important issues that always plagued Raju is the nature of I-consciousness.[1] He attached utmost importance to it. In the preface to his *Structural Depths of Indian Thought* (1985), Raju addresses the reader as follows: "Many doctrines may be found by the reader to have loose ends; but I hope to tie them together (God willing) in a future work on philosophy of the 'I am'. Readers may do the same in their own way. The 'I am' has become nothing or nothingness not only for most existentialists but also to the followers of Wittgenstein and analytical philosophers of the present. But it is more positive to human existence and more valuable to it than nature which man faces."[2]

Raju traces back I-consciousness (I-AM) to the *Bṛhadāraṇyaka Upaniṣad* and the *Bible.* In the above *Upaniṣad* it is mentioned: "Originally this (universe) was only Ātman in the form of a person. He looked around and saw Nothing besides him. For he uttered 'I am'.

Out of it arose the word 'I'. Therefore, when one is aske "who are you" he says first: 'I am', and then adds his other name."[3] Similarly, in the *Bible* one comes across the statement: "So God created man in his own image; in the image of God he him, ..."[4] and further mentioned: " And God said to Moses, I AM THAT I AM, and he said, Thus shalt thou say unto the children of Israel I AM hath sent me unto you."[5] What Raju intends to highlight here is that I am as a self-affirming principle must be reviewed in order to make it center of one's philosophical thinking. If it is treated as 'nothing', then who is it that affirms its 'nothingness'? This becomes a fundamental question for Raju in his treatment of the nature of I-consciousness. The simple way to establish its (I-consciousness's) existence is to invoke the principle of non-contradiction here. One who affirms in order to declare that it is 'nothing' must be self-conscious and cannot be in a position to treat himself as 'nothing'. In a way he is the 'I am'. Raju goes to an extent of saying that in the absence of I am: "the structure of time, space, universals etc., cannot be intelligible..."[6] The I am, which is relegated to obscurity as meaningless in the history of philosophy provides meaning to the very history of philosophy. This serves as a major backdrop for our discussion on the proposed subject.

An Inquiry into the Being

A cursory look at the history of philosophy, both eastern and western, reveals that philosophers of the past and the present made sincere attempts to inquire into the nature of the Being. The ancient Greek monist Parmenides held that there are two important ways of inquiry. The first confirms that whatever is Being: "is and cannot not-be is -not". This is the legitimate path of truth that makes us realize that the Being is one and cannot be created, destroyed, or changed. If any one of these alterations is possible within the Being, then the Being would no longer be what 'is and would become what 'is not'. But by definition there is no 'is not' from which Being could come into existence or into which being could change. Being is one seamless immutable whole. The other way of inquiry is only a path of opinion which claims that something arises from not-being.[7] Similarly, for Aristotle, the question of Being is the first and foremost for any philosophical investigation. But, Aristotle's inquiry stops short of the scientific conception of the Being, which is interested in the first principles and the causes of the various sciences. Taking the cue from Aristotle, Martin Heidegger in his work *Being and Time* (1927) made a valiant attempt to understand the nature and meaning of the Being. Accordingly, he claims that his basic concern is to probe into the 'fundamental ontology' as against the 'metaphysics of presence' or 'logo-centrism'. Unlike the former, which is concerned with the very nature of the Being, the latter is primarily concerned with the Being in its classificatory mode. Of course, in his later work *An Introduction to Metaphysics* (1935) Heidegger moved away from 'fundamental ontology' to 'history of Being' in order to stress on human participation in the process or happening of Being. Coming to analytic tradition, early Wittgenstein ruled out the presence of the philosophical 'I' in the world of things. According to him, 'I' is an error in grammar. In other words, it is a grammatical illusion. This does not mean that Wittgenstein repudiated the notion of 'I', rather he accommodated it in the realm of 'what cannot be said'. Once Wittgenstein remarked that his *Tractatus Logico-Philosopicus* (1921) became popular not because of what is written in it, but for what is not said in it.

Raju's Fundamental Ontology

For Raju, Being manifests itself in the form of I-consciousness. It has both ontic[8] and ontological existence. In his introduction to his book *Spirit Being and Self: Studies in Indian and Western Philosophy*, Raju writes that he started understanding the very spirit of the *Upaniṣadic* tradition in India, and also the grand tradition of the West. They provided him with great insights into the nature of I am. In fact, Raju acknowledges the importance of the idea of I am as I think presented in the philosophy of Descartes in the context of epistemology. However, Descartes' analysis of I am in the context of arriving at epistemological certainty, according to Raju, has ontological implications too, for it is also a search for something in which all thinking and cognition can be located. Otherwise Descartes could not have been certain that the 'I think' is automatic, although he used 'therefore' I am. The variety of interpretations of his *cogito* made his intention vague and carried the general impression that he was trying to show the certainty of the subject as against that of object. In other words, the existence of the object is secondary or derivative. Therefore, claims Raju, Descartes should have said "I am (exist), therefore I think". In the assertion

"I think, therefore I am" it is the second 'I'that comprehends both subjective/objective/empirical I and also its acts.[9]

The I-consciousness, which is also referred to as the Self or existential consciousness, as opposed to phenomenological consciousness or ego-consciousness or attributive consciousness, is conscious of its own being. In other words, the I-consciousness is the indication for the presence of the Self. To put it in the words of Raju: "The 'I' is never experienced by anyone without the 'am', If the 'I' is true, then 'am' must be true. There is no 'I' without the 'am' and no 'am' without the 'I'."[10] This statement of Raju highlights that 'I' as the self is inseparable from "am" which its being. In short, 'I' and 'am' are inseparable from each other.

According to Raju, the additional epistemological approaches to the I-consciousness can be summarized in the following way. In epistemology, normally knowledge situation involves three important factors, *viz.,* subject, object, and the consciousness of the object in question. When a person sees a rose, he simply claims that "I see the rose" or "I am conscious of the rose" or "I have consciousness of the rose". Thus we have three terms in the form of 'I', its consciousness of the object, and the object in question. Thus knowledge is a three termed relation. However, we come across certain reductionist tendencies wherein these three terms are reduced to two or even to one.[11]In the case of two termed relation, the 'I' is identified with the process of knowing or of being conscious of something. Thus the 'I' is denied independent existence. In such cases, when someone says that "I see the rose", I am not affirming myself, but only the consciousness of the rose and the rose. This is precisely the position adopted by Hume and his followers in the west, and the Vijňānavādins in the east. Further Raju holds that the two-factor theory considers the 'I' as an appearance or deposit of consciousness. Therefore, the 'I' is neither a substantive nor a noun nor a pronoun. Here in this context Raju makes a distinction between the claims that "I am conscious of rose" and "I am the consciousness of the rose". In the case of the former the 'I' as a subject is conscious of the rose. This consciousness can be termed as phenomenological consciousness or ego-consciousness.; whereas in the case of the latter the consciousness of the rose is rooted in the I am, which is the existential consciousness.

Coming to the reduction of three factors into one, in the Indian context it is the Vijñānavāda school of Buddhism that reduced everything to a form of consciousness. First it reduced the 'I' to the very process of consciousness, and then reduced the external objects to consciousness. Such a position is often termed as subjectivism, but according to Raju, this is not right label for there is no subject involved in such a position. Instead he suggests "consciousness-is" as an alternative label.[12]

Now Raju tries to examine the consequences of these positions. Of the three, the first two, namely, epistemological triadism, and epistemological dualism, are influential. Of these two, the epistemological dualism, claims Raju, cannot explain the possibility of epistemological error and illusion. For instance, one may mistake "X" for "Y", and says: "That is a Y". Later he discovers his mistake and says: "That is an X", but not "Y". In this case one has to make a distinction between the consciousness of 'X' and that of 'Y'. The latter cannot realize the mistake committed in seeing 'Y'. Therefore, there is a need for consciousness, which can assert: "I know that I saw a Y, but it is really X". Such a consciousness must continuous and also must be self-conscious. In this statement, he first 'I' transcends the second 'I'. In this context, Raju makes us realize that there is no solipsism at the epistemological level, for the knowing subject necessarily presupposes something that is to be known. In other words, the epistemological/empirical 'I' assumes significance only in the context of the other existents.

Further Raju makes a distinction between the existential consciousness and the phenomenological consciousness on the basis of their intentional nature. In a sense both are intentional, but the intentionality of the former is directed towards the inner or inwards; while the intentionality of the latter towards the outer or outwards. One can say that I am the existential consciousness, I have the phenomenological consciousness.[13] In fact, Raju analyzes the approaches of abnormal/depth psychology to consciousness as a philosopher, but not as a psychoanalyst. He takes into consideration the attempts made by both Freud and Jung in understanding the human psyche. According to Freud, consciousness belongs to the conscious part of human personality. Below this layer of consciousness, there is pre-conscious, and still below it lies the unconsciousness. Freud held that the ego is the coherent organization of the various mental episodes. However, the whole of it is not conscious. In fact, the ego is the combination of conscious, pre-conscious and unconscious. Freud technically called the unconscious state of the ego the *id.* The pure *id* contains only instincts, but the conscious ego possesses reason. But Freud did not separate the conscious ego from the *id.* In other words, the conscious ego being the part of the *id* shareswith all the three states, namely, conscious, pre-conscious, and unconscious.[14] According to Raju, Freud's explanation is not clear, for he identifies the *id* with the unconscious ego.

Another important feature that is to be noticed in the Freudian abnormal psychology is that every individual has two primary instincts, namely, the life instinct and the death instinct. The former is the sex instinct and the latter is the ego instinct.[15] But, Raju notices that we generally identifythe ego instinct with the life instinct or the instinct of the "am". But for Freud, the instinct to conserve oneself is the instinct to regress to inanimate nature. Therefore, it is the death instinct. The point that Raju wants to drive home here is that in Freud's abnormal psychology the ego, normal or abnormal, is the result of an integration of certain mental processes. It is not the "I am" (self-consciousness). The Freudian ego is the product of conscious and unconscious processes. The most interesting thing is that the ego-consciousness is rooted in the unconscious *id.* To put it in other words, the conscious ego is the *id* that becomes conscious and rational due to its exposure to the external world. Now Raju raises the question: are the conscious and unconscious out of which the ego-structure of personality develops, impersonal? Prior to the formation of ego-consciousness, there must be something to witness these processes. Since ego-consciousness, according to Freud, is rooted in the unconscious, the latter cannot be its *noema,*[16] or the object of phenomenological reduction. According to Raju, the consciousness that witnesses all these processes is the "I am or I-consciousness". To quote Raju's remarks here: "the self-conscious I am" must be present in both the normal and abnormal persons. The ego is its *noema.* Then why does it get distorted in abnormal cases? We have to say that just the ego has its identification with its objects and distorted ego-ideals, the "I am" has its identifications with such egos."[17]

Turning to Jung's psychology, Raju holds that 'I am' is absent even in his psychology except in the third person of persona and the ego. Like Freud, Jung also maintained that conscious and unconscious are the main principles for ego. In fact, the ego is present in both of them. In other words, the ego is partly conscious and partly unconscious. Unlike the ego, the psyche, for Jung, is the totality of both conscious and unconscious. The ego with both its conscious and unconscious parts is the 'I'. But the persona as a specific form of general psychic behavior to the external world is wider than the ego. It is a function -complex and is concerned with the object. According to Jung, it is a: "compromise between the individual and society."[18] It means that the general psyche of individual as the collective unity of conscious and unconscious constitutes the very human personality. However, Raju points out that the 'I am' as self-asserting principle is missing in Jung's psychology. As a matter of fact, Jung's analysis of personality applies to both normal and abnormal cases. The individual is a total person, and that is the Self. But, the Self cannot be an object of consciousness, for it is self-conscious. Only ego is the object of consciousness. According to Raju, Jung's psychology is rooted in philosophy for it recognizes the unity of conscious and unconscious in persona. This position of Jung comes closer to the Advaitic concept of *jīva.*

But the question remains, where do we locate I am in Jung's psychology? Jung claimed that the ego is known. But by whom is it known? The ego as a *noema* must belong to a transcendental self. Jung did not explain the nature of the transcendence. The ego remains an ego until its self-transcendence is realized. Another problem with Jung's psychology is that it tries to extricate the conscious from the unconscious and calls the latter the Mother. In fact, it is other way round. The unconscious is rooted in the conscious. An empirical self is the amalgamation of the both conscious and unconscious. It is by means of realization the unconscious transforms itself into the conscious by making the Self as pure I-consciousness.

But, how can one establish that there is Self (Ātman) in the form of pure I-consciousness? In order to answer this question Raju analyzes the nature of 'I' as illustrated in the *Taittirīya Upaniṣad.* According to this *Upaniṣad,* there are various forms of self-identification. They are forms of ego development, according to Raju. For instance, when the self is identified with body-sense complex, the assertions about its identification take the forms like, "I am the body", "I am the life in the body", "I am the perceiver of the rose", "I am the thinker". In all these cases 'I' is known through its identifications, but not in isolation from them. In order to know the real nature of the 'I', we need to have an experience in which the 'I' as pure 'I-consciousness' is free from all these identifications. Such an experience is identified and well defined in the *Māndūkya Upaniṣad* in the form of triple stream of experience (*avastātraya-vicāra*). The three important states of the 'I' are waking (*jāgṛt*), dream (*svapna*) and deep sleep (*suṣupti*). These states ultimately lead to a fourth state, which is an absolute (*turīya*) state. Well, Raju is very realistic when he says that we do not know much about the fourth state, but one cannot deny experiencing the first three. How do these three states of experience disclose the nature of the I-consciousness? Raju maintains that these three states not only reveal who "I am", but also "what "I am". The philosophical significance of these three states of experience is not recognized by many a thinker for they are normal everyday occurrences. In their attempt to analyze the nature of unconscious, the depth psychologists have analyzed the state of dream, but not the state of deep sleep. What is wrong with depth psychology is, opines Raju, that it did not realize that the unconscious in its massive form is present only in deep sleep state.

In the waking and dream states, the 'I' is intentional in its nature, for its intentionality is directed towards the objects of real and dream worlds respectively. Although these two worlds are different, there is some sort of continuity in the I-consciousness. In the waking state the 'I' is associated with mind, body, and sense-organs. In the dream state the body and the sense-organs are withdrawn. But in the state of deep sleep, mind, body and sense-organs are withdrawn. In the waking state one is able to identify the objects the world of his/her experience. Similar is the case with the state of dream. An individual is able to identify the objects of his/her dream world. But in the deep sleep state nothing is experienced, yet when the person wakes up from his/her deep sleep, he/she is able to say: "I had a sound sleep". If one's body, mind, and sense-organs are completely withdrawn, then how is it possible for a person to say: "I had a sound sleep?" Who is that which witnesses this state of experience? This is fundamental philosophical question. This question leads us to fundamental ontology or the nature of "I-consciousness". As such the I-consciousness as "I am" is present in all the three states, but in the first two states its presence is not realized. It is only in the state of deep sleep its presence is noticed. Although the deep sleep state is permeated by the unconscious, the presence of 'I' as the self-conscious principle makes one remember one's deep sleep condition.[19]

Concluding Remarks

P.T. Raju as one of the finest exponents of Advaita in the contemporary times has established, beyond doubt, the significance of I-consciousness. This is the fundamental principle which transcends the objects of experience both in waking and dream states. The arguments presented by Raju unequivocally prove that I-consciousness is the fundamental ontology of Advaita. All other forms of conscious states derive their being only from that fundamental principle. In the absence of such a fundamental principle there exists no knowledge of anything of this world of facts of existence. What is called intentional or phenomenological consciousness derives its being only from the I-consciousness or existential consciousness.

Notes

* I express my deep sense of gratitude to late Professor R.Balasubramanian for introducing me to Advaita Vedānta.

1. In P.T.Raju's philosophy, the expressions "I-consciousness", "I", "I am" "Self-consciousness", "Self", and "Existential Consciousness", "Witness Consciousness" represent the same supreme principle, the Ātman.
2. P.T. Raju, *Structural Depths of Indian Thought* (New Delhi: South Asia Publishers, 1985), p. xii.
3. *Bṛhadāraṇyaka Upaniṣad,* 1.4.1.
4. *The Bible,* (*Genesis*), 1.2.
5. *Ibid., (Exodus),* III.14.
6. P.T. Raju, *Structural Depths of Indian Thought,* p. xii.
7. Forrest E. Baird and Walter Kaufman, *Ancient Philosophy* (New Jearsy: Prentice-Hall, 1996), 2nd edn., p. 20.
8. This is the expression used by Martin Heidegger for Being per se. According to him, Being is ontically prior to its ontological existence.

9. P.T. Raju, *Spirit, Being and Self: Studies in Indian and Western Philosophy* (New Delhi: South Asia Publishers, 1982), p. 5.
10. P.T. Raju, "Approaches to I-consciousness: Its Depth, Normal, and abnormal, " in his *Spirit, Being and Self: Studies in Indian and Western Philosophy,* p. 242.
11. *Ibid.,* p. 243.
12. *Ibid.,* p. 244.
13. *Ibid.,* p. 245.
14. *Ibid.,* p. 246.
15. Sigmund Freud, *Beyond the Pleasure Principle,* Eng. Trans., J. M. Hubback (London: International Psycho-Analytic Press, 1922), p. 54.
16. This terminology was coined by Edmund Husserl to refer to the objects of phenomenological reduction. Raju makes use of this expression to show that the Self as I-consciousness cannot be a *noema.*
17. Approaches to I-consciousness: Its Depth, Normal, and abnormal, " in his *Spirit, Being and Self: Studies in Indian and Western Philosophy,* p. 248.
18. Jolande Jacobi, *The Psychology of C.G.Jung*, Eng. trans, K.W. Bash, New Haven:Yale University Press, 1954, p. 24.
19. P.T. Raju, "Approaches to I-consciousness: Its Depth, Normal, and abnormal," in his *Spirit, Being and Self: Studies in Indian and Western Philosophy,* p. 252.

7

Is Self-Knowledge Possible?

Introduction

Before we undertake any examination of the possibility of self-knowledge we need to address two fundamental questions. They are: 1. What is self? 2.Is self embodied or disembodied? Philosophers in the East and West made sincere and valiant attempts to explain the notion of self.For instance, the entire classical Indian philosophical tradition, broadly speaking, is classified into two major streams called *anātmavādins* and *ātmavādins*. The former subscribe to the position that there is no substantial and continuous self, and what is called self is a mere collection of aggregates (*skandhas*) and is coextensive with body. On the contrary, the latter subscribe to the position that there is an independent and continuous self that is disembodied and its coexistence with body is only accidental. The debate between the philosophers belonging to these two streams concerning the nature of self is tenacious. Buddhism and Advaita are two prominent classical Indian philosophical traditions which are often locked in this debate. The notion of self further leads us to the distinction between empirical or psychological-I (*jīva*) and the philosophical-I. The knowledge of the former and its method of knowing are completely different from that of the latter. The empirical or psychological-I has mere phenomenal existence, whereas the philosophical-I has absolute or trans-phenomenal existence. In the final analysis, the debate between phenomenalists and absolutists boils down to the ontological status of self and the possibility of knowledge of such self. In this essay an attempt is made to highlight the salient features of the debate between Buddhist phenomenalism and Advaitic absolutism.

Buddhist Notion of No-Self *(anattā)*

In our day-to-day life we frequently use the expression 'self' to refer to our own identity. Therefore, individual identity and self are used synonymously. Perhaps Buddhism does not oppose such a self which is identified with empirical or psychological-I. The death of empirical or psychological-I necessitates the death of self (*ātman or attā*). In other words, the self of Buddhism is only a temporal entity but not an eternal transcendental entity that finds its immanence in human body. Then it makes sense to say that Buddhism is not really averse to using the expression 'self' insofar as it refers to the identity of a mortal individual. The empirical or psychological-I which is made of aggregates (*skandhas*) is subjected to dependent origination. Often the critics of Buddhism hold that if there is no self then there is no meaning in talking about *karma*, rebirth and *Nirvāṇa.* These notions have any meaning only in the context of an existing self.

But Buddhism derives its no-self theory from the Doctrine of Dependent Origination (*pratītyasamutpāda*). This doctrine shatters the belief that there exists an eternal or a permanent entity that is variously called soul or self or spirit in every individual. Even the great religions of the world such as Judaism, Christianity, Islam, Jainism, and Hinduism and the great philosophers such as Socrates, Plato, Descartes and Kant acknowledged soul/self as an eternal or immortal substance.[1] Although the human body is subjected to change and decay, the soul/self that resides in human beings is abiding and immutable. It is the soul/self that animates the body. However, it is completely distinct from body for it is spiritual. The Vedāntins call it Ātman.[2] Contrary to this view, Buddhism does not admit any permanent and enduring entity called soul/self in human beings. The Doctrine of Dependent Origination teaches us that everything is dependent on something else and conditional. The world of existence is a testimony to the Doctrine of Dependent Origination. Nothing in this world is permanent and unchanging. According to Buddhism, if one deeply enters into one's recesses and examine whether he or she could aware of any unchanging entity called soul or self, all that one could encounter is nothing more than a sensation, an impression, a perception, an image, a feeling, an impulse and so on, but never an entity called soul or self. This view of Buddhism is almost echoed in the writings of David Hume when he held:

> For my part, when I enter most intimately into what I call 'myself', I always stumble on some particular perception or other, of heat or cold, light or shade, love or hatred, pain or pleasure. I never catch 'myself' at any time without a perception, and can never observe anything but the perception.[3]

However, it needs to be clarified here that there are certain fundamental differences between their philosophical orientations. Buddhism is primarily a philosophy of action while the philosophy of Hume is fundamentally interested in establishing the doctrine of sensationalism. According to Buddhism, the human body is composed of five aggregates (*skandhas*). They are: form (matter), feeling (pleasant, unpleasant, neutral), perceptions (all the five senses), mental formations or impulses (greed, hatred, etc.), and consciousness.[4] None of the above mentioned *skandhas* is identified with self. Similarly, the totality of the aggregates does not provide us with any permanent self. To think that the totality of the aggregates gives rise to self is to live in illusion. Every *skandha* is subjected to the Doctrine of Dependent Origination. And these *skandhas* are neither material nor spiritual in nature. Our physical form is the result of these *skandhas,* and it may be called empirical or psychological-I that is subjected to constant change. This changing self is the result of our linguistic habits and psychological factors. We often refer to our own identity as 'I' or self (linguistically) and this 'I' is also associated with certain psychological factors such as craving, grasping, insecurity, and fear of death.

The tricky issues that follow from the above description of composition of human being are continuity and unity of experience of an individual, more importantly, *karma* and rebirth. How does Buddhism account for these issues? If human being is a conglomerate of ever changing aggregates (*skandhas*), then what is it that is reborn? Is law of *karma* a valid doctrine in the context of the Buddhist view of non-abiding self? How can we ascribe personal identity to any individual? How do we explain the transformation of a child to an adult? If there is no abiding self, then we cannot hold an individual responsible for his or her actions. Whom are we going to attribute praise or blame, reward or punishment? If there is no enduring or continuous self then the individual who committed a crime at t_1 is not the same at t_2. The doctrine of *anattāvāda* of Buddhism, somehow, does not fix any moral responsibility on any individual for there is no enduring self to take it on itself. (In fact, these are the questions put by King Miḷinda to the well-known Buddhist monk Nāgasena.[5]

But the issues raised by critics can be satisfactorily answered by Buddhism without giving up its *anattāvāda*. Of course, the analogy of a chain of links would help us in understanding the Buddhist position. The chain is treated as one single continuous unit, but each link is externally connected to the other. There is no internal link between one link and the other. In the similar fashion, all our experiences are continuous and their unity is due to the cause and effect relation that we see in successive experiences. To take the example of flame produced by a candle, the flame is continuous but there is nothing that persists in flame from one moment to another. Yet, we see flame as a continuous phenomenon. Also, the flame of one candle can also light another one. Does it mean that the second fame is due to some persistent entity? The flame of the candle is caused by certain extraneous factors. These factors are different from the flame which is their outcome. The unbroken succession of causal events enables continuous existence of flame, although the two flames are different. The purport of these analogies is that we can account for our continuity and unity of experience (apperception) without postulating any mysterious permanent entity called self. The feeling of one's own continuity and unity of experience results from various stets constituting our experience from unbroken succession of causes and effects in accordance with the Doctrine of Dependent Origination. Even the *kārmic* particles that accrued during our life of *saṁsāra* cause our present life whish their effect. Thus there is no transmigration of self/soul from body to another. The past is the cause of the present, and the present is the cause of the future. Thus Buddhism disapproves the existence of permanent or abiding self.

According to Buddhism, consciousness is neither an entity nor something permanent. It is an unbroken continuous stream. Similar view is echoed by William James nearly after twenty five hundred years later. To quote him in this context:

> For twenty years past I have mistrusted 'consciousness' as an entity....To deny plumply that 'consciousness' exists seems so absurd on the face of it-----for undeniably 'thoughts' do exist ---that I fear some readers will follow me no further. Let me then immediately explain that I mean only to deny that the word stands for an entity, but to insist most emphatically that it does stand for a function.[6]

Compare the above statement of James with the following statement of Buddhism:

> Misery only doth exist, none miserable.
>
> No doer is there; naught save the deed is found.
>
> Nirvāṇa is, but not the man who seeks it.
>
> The path exists, but not the traveller on it.[7]

It is the continuous stream of consciousness but not any other entity that provides link between our past and present, and our present and future. Thus moral responsibility poses no problem to the doctrine of *anattā.* An individual is held responsible for his/her actions not because he/she possesses a permanent self but because his/her existence is an unbroken stream of causal connections in which his/her past, present and future are bound together. Therefore, the ontology of Buddhism does not contradict its ethical discipline. The doctrine of *anattā* does no damage to the moral realm of individuals.

Advaita Notion of Self (*ātman*)

Advaita, contrary to Buddhist view, admits permanent and abiding self that exists independent of human body. Its association with human body is termed as bondage. Thus it becomes enworlded subjectivity. Following the tradition of *Upaniṣads,* Advatins advocate the view that self is a conscious principle and it is distinct from mind (*manas/ antahkaraṇa*). The former is spiritual and the latter corporeal. Therefore, self can never be reduced to mind. The self is a basic residue that the individual (*jīva*) experiences when he or she gets behind all mental functions called *vṛttis,* which can be objectified. According to Advaita, self-realization (self-knowledge) is literally possible. The possibility and desirability of such an experience forms the crux of Advaita. Mind, unlike the self, belongs to lower order of reality and is the connecting link between the self and world of nature. If this distinction between the self and mind is not noticed then the psychology of orthodox Indian philosophical traditions cannot be understood.

What we call human personality or ego (empirical-I) is associated with mind-body-sense complex. This empirical-I possesses reflective thinking for it is conditioned by mind. The nature of mind is more understood from within. It is the inward approach that makes the subject of experience completely conscious of its own actions. This inward approach can be called variously as intuition, self-reflection and introspection. Mind being a part of physical body cannot exist independent of it. But in the west, especially in the writings of Descartes, mind is treated as a spiritual entity whose attribute is thinking in contrast to body whose attribute is extension. Descartes identified mind in its pure form with pure-ego (disembodied self). Such an approach to mind is not acceptable to Advaita. Excepting Cārvāka and Buddhism, all other systems of Indian philosophy treat self and mind as two distinct entities representing the higher and lower levels of world order. The self as pure consciousness operates through mind (*manas*).[8] In a way, the activities of mind come to a complete halt if it is not associated with the self. Thus the basic epistemic activities of human beings hat involve reflective thinking are possible only due to the presence of the conscious principle called the self. The mind which is believed to be the conscious principle responsible for cognitions and conations in general is only a medium or instrument.

The dictum 'know thy self' becomes important in the present context. As reflective individuals we make use of our reason to ascertain the knowledge about the things of the empirical world. But reflection as essence of reason is something inward or internal. Although it is treated as an operation of mind, yet mind's operations are prompted by the presence of consciousness. This consciousness which operates through mind is not the essential property of mind, but only its accidental property. The self, which is the innermost essence of human beings, is described in the *Chāndogya Upaniṣad* in the following manner:

> The self *(ātman)* which is free from evil, free from old age, free from death, free from grief, free from hunger and thirst, whose desire is the real, whose thoughts are true, he should be sought. Him, one should desire to understand. He who has found out and understands that self; he obtains all worlds and desires.[9]

Therefore, the search for this ultimate metaphysical principle called the self is essentially a matter of going deeper and deeper into the very foundations of human existence.

In the third, fourth and fifth *mantras* of the *Māndūkya Upaniṣad*[10] we come across the interesting interpretation about the nature of self through the triple stream of experience (*avasthā-traya-vicāra).* These three states of experience are waking (*jāgrat),* dream (*śvapna*), and deep sleep (*suṣupti*). According to this *Upaniṣad,* the self as conscious principle is present in all the three states. A person can narrate his/her experiences only when he/she is conscious of them. In order to be conscious of one's experiences a person must possess consciousness. The self as a conscious principle is called *Vaiśvānara* in waking state. In this state the consciousness is intentional for it is always directed towards something or other. Therefore, we know consciousness as consciousness of this or that object. The mind-sense complex is the aid or instrument to through which the consciousness functions operates to experience the objects of gross nature.

In the dream state, in spite of the fact that senses are at rest, mind functions. Even in this state consciousness is intentional for it is directed or oriented towards the objects of dream that are nothing but the impressions of our day-to-day experience deposited in the mind. These impressions are projected by mind. Consciousness in this state is called *Taijasa.*

In the deep-sleep state, along with senses the mind is also withdrawn. A person who undergoes deep-sleep does not experience any object, internal or external, gross or subtle. But when he wakes up from the state of deep-sleep he simply states, "I slept well".In other words, he did not know anything. There was no object presented to his/her consciousness. The absence of consciousness does not mean the non-existence of consciousness. It is present all through in the form of *Prājña,* for otherwise the person who experienced deep-sleep would not have uttered, "I slept well". The following quote from the *Māṅḍūkya Upaniṣad* further illustrates the deep sleep experience.

> That state is deep sleep where the sleeper does not desire any enjoyable thing, and does not see any dream. The third quarter is Prajña whose sphere is deep-sleep, who remains one and undifferentiated who is a mass of mere consciousness who is full of bliss who experiences bliss, and who is the doorway to the experience(of the dream and waking states).[11]

What is interesting to note in this analysis of the self is that distinguishes deep-sleep state from other two states of experience. Unlike in waking and dream states, there are no objects to be presented to the consciousness in the deep-sleep state. The self in this state is one and, unified and undifferentiated. In other words, it is non-relational and non-intentional. The state of deep sleep can be termed as bliss, which is the true nature of the self. However, this state of bliss is not permanent as the state of deep sleep is not permanent. The self as conscious principle is present in all the three states. These three states of experience are transcended by the fourth state called *turīya.*The real nature of the self is known only in this state. The self as conscious principle transcends the ontological, theological, and other limitations. Therefore, it cannot be described positively as this or that.

Similarly, in the *Taittirīya Upaniṣad*[12] we come across an interesting analysis of the self as conscious principle. The empirical self or human personality is composed of five sheaths (*kośas*). They are---- the sheath of matter (*annamaya-kośa*), the sheath of life (*prāṇamaya-kośa*), the sheath of conscious activity (*manomaya-kośa),* the sheath of intelligence (*vijñānamaya-kośa)*, and the sheath of bliss (*ānandamaya-kośa).* Each succeeding sheath is a self of the preceding sheath that forms its body. So far as psychological-I is concerned the sheath of matter is responsible for physical and gross body, and the sheath of life for the five sense-organs of action and the five vital airs (*prāṇas).* The sheath of conscious activity is responsible for five organs of sense and the sheath of intelligence for intellect (*buddhi)* and five sense organs. The sheath of bliss is responsible for the individual *avidyā* disassociated from the bodily and mental functions. The self is enveloped by all these five sheaths. Out of these, the first sheath consists of gross body (*sthūla-śārīra*), the second, third, and fourth constitute subtle body (*sūkṣma-śārīra*), and the fifth causal body *(kāraṇa- śārīra).* The purport of this analysis is to show that the self as conscious principle cannot be equated with matter, life, mind, and intellect. It is "different from and within that which consists of the understanding of the self, consisting of bliss."[13]

In the *Kena Upaniṣad,* the inquiry into the nature of the self takes the form of a search for an ultimate agent or doer of human activity. It is asked: "By whom willed and directed does the mind light on its objects? By whom commanded does life the first, move? At whose will do(people) utter the speech? And what God is it that prompts the eye and the ear?"[14] All these questions are answered with an emphatic assertion that there is a basic self that instructs the eye to colour, the ear to sound the understanding of consciousness. And this self is "other than known and other than unknown."[15] The most important of the questions asked above is the question: What is that which directs all the human activities? It is not easy to answer this question as "the eye goes not, speech goes not nor the mind; we know not we understand not how one can teach this."[16] Since the self is not an object known to the human subject, it cannot be apprehended by the eye, ear, and reason. It is the ultimate subject. It cannot be known, but can only be realized in total self-consciousness. This self is self-luminous. As an ultimate revealing principle of the presence and absence of objects, it is transcendentally *a priori,* and is known as the subject, but not in the sense of 'knower' or'cognizer'(*jńāta or pramāta*). It is a permanent subject. Anything other than the self is only an object. In the language of Wittgenstein (see foot-note) it can be called the 'metaphysical subject or I'. What is most striking in the above analysis of the self is that the self as conscious principle is to be distinguished from the psychological or empirical-I, which is bound by the limitations (*upādhis*) such as mind-body-sense complex.

In contrast to the metaphysical-I, psychological or empirical-I is termed as human personality or ego. It is treated as a secondary subject since it is opposed to all that is external to it. It is endowed with cognitive power because of its proximity to the ever-conscious principle (the self). The secondary subject is also referred to as internal organ (*antahkaraṇa*). Depending upon its functions it is variously called mind (*manas*), intellect (*buddhi*), ego (*ahaṁkāra*), and the memory stuff (*citta*). Although the internal organ is a single unit, its functions are four-fold. The function of *manas*is to doubt, analyze, or synthesize whether it is this or that object. The function of *buddhi* is to make an assertion about the status of the object perceived. For instance, the judgment 'This is a horse' is the result of the decision of *buddhi.* The function of *ahaṁkāra* is to attribute 'I-ness, and that of *citta* is to present the given sense-experience in an unified apperceptive mass. When an object is perceived, *manas* assumes the form of the object in question and offers it to *buddhi.* In turn, *buddhi* offers it to *citta.* Finally, *ahaṁkāra* appropriates it as a form of its own perception. Such a mechanism reveals the dynamic nature of the internal organ[17] The knowledge obtained by the functions of the internal organ can be communicated, for there is a subject in the form of psychological or empirical-I to communicate it. And our day-to-day ordinary language is so designed for this purpose. Our knowledge at this level is rational. Therefore, every linguistic expression that we make represents whatever is grasped by our intellect through the internal organ. But, behind all these functions there is the self or the transcendental-I. The knowledge obtained by the internal organ is finite, incidental, relative, transient, mediate and informative. The knowledge by mediation is empirical, pragmatic, and always presupposes subject-object polarity.

The secondary subject or human personality or ego is part and parcel of this world of actions. The secondary subject is a combination of spiritual and material elements. The material element in secondary subject obscures its spiritual element. The result is that the secondary subject is dragged into the world of action and is lured by the things of the world.

Concluding Remarks

From the above analysis of self it is clear that the positions of Buddhism and Advaita are diametrically opposed to each other. The former advocates the view that there is no indwelling and abiding self over and above human personality or psychological-I that is composed of aggregates (*skandhas*). According to the latter, there is an indwelling, abiding self that is eternal and spiritual. Advaita criticises the standpoint of Buddhism on the ground that if psychological or empirical-I is made up of aggregates that are fleeting and momentary, then a series of aggregates cannot account for its own existence and functions. Similarly, the followers of Buddhism attack Advaita position by holding the view that it is not the abiding or permanent self that is responsible for making the statement "I slept well' once a person undergoes deep-sleep. The mind which is at rest during the deep-sleep state can also prompt the psychological or empirical-I to make such a statement for the statement is an empty statement. In other words, the statement 'I slept well' means I did not know anything during that state. To utter such a statement, Advaita need not posit the existence of permanent or transcendental self. However, both Buddhism and Advaita admit psychological or empirical-I. For the former, the personal identity is attributed to a group of aggregates and for the latter personal identity is attributed to a psycho-physical entity called *jīva*. Insofar as the knowledge of psychological or empirical-I is concerned both admit knowledge of such a self is possible. Although one does not find much discussion about the way in which the knowledge of psychological or empirical-I in Buddhism and Advaita, they do not reject reflection as a source of such knowledge. Does such knowledge, strictly speaking, qualify as knowledge at all? As Wittgenstein aptly remarked, the first person claim to knowledge is not a claim at all for it can never be false. To say that "I know this is my right hand" is not a claim to knowledge. At the most it can be treated as an assertion made by a person out of his own self-scanning or self-monitoring. Locke held that intuitively we know about our own self. As held by Susan Stebbing the knowledge of one's own physical and mental states can be characterized as non-observational knowledge. According to Stuart Hampshire, such knowledge can be treated as non-propositional kind for it can never be characterised as false. Self-referential statements are generally treated as avowals. One does not find subject-object dichotomy in such self-referential statements. Even if one attributes one's privileged access to such a form of experience yet such experience does not qualify as knowledge in the public domain for it is not accessible to others to judge the veracity of such experience(s). The neo-expressivist view on self-knowledge trades between epistemic and constitutivist views on first person authority. For instance, someone utters "I have terrible headache", "I am so tired". These utterances refer to one's own physical and mental states. Verificationists may find it unconvincing to accept them as part of epistemic knowledge. However, we cannot simply ignore such personal experiences and references to such personal experiences though our ordinary language as highlighted by later Wittgenstein. The existence of external (objective) world certainly presupposes the existence of internal (subjective) world. The method or methods of knowing external world cannot be used as a yardstick to gauge the internal world. Perhaps, Buddhism and Advaita do not face such a problem as they accept contemplation as a legitimate approach to know what is internal. Objectivity alone cannot be the criterion to justify our knowledge claims.

Notes

1. F.C. Copleston, *A History of Philosophy*, New York: Doubleday & Co., 1966, vols. I, IV, & VI).
2. *Kaṭha Upaniṣad* II.18.
3. David Hume, *A Treatise on Human Nature,* L.A. Selby-Bigge (ed.), New York: OUP, 1951, p. 252.
4. *Samyutta-Nikāya,* III, 127-28 (Texts), p. 74.
5. *Miḷindapanha,* 71, trans., 234-38.
6. William James, "Does Consciousness Exist?" in *Essays in Radical Empiricism and a Pluralistic Universe,* London: Longman's Gren & Co., 1904, pp. 1-38.
7. *Visuddhi-Magga,* Ch. XVI, trans., p. 146.
8. M. Hiriyanna, *Indian Philosophy of Values*, Mysore: Kavyalaya Publishers, 1975, p. 28.
9. *Chāndogya Upaniṣad,* 7.7.1. in S. Radhakrishnan (tr.), *The Principal Upaniṣads*, London: Allen and Unwin, 1953.
10. *Māndūkya Upaniṣad* 3.4.5.
11. *Ibid.,* p. 5.
12. *Taittirīya Upaniṣad,* 2.
13. *Ibid.,* 2.5.1.
14. *Kena Upaniṣad,* 8.
15. *Ibid.,* 14.
16. *Ibid.,* 13.
17. P.T.Raju, "Nature of Mind and Its Activities," in Haridas Bhattacharya (ed.), *Cultural Heritage of India,* Calcutta: The Ramakrishna Institute of Indian Culture, 1983, p. 507.

8

Salient Features of Śrī Rāmānuja's Qualified Non-Dualism

> If Viśiṣṭādvaita can be likened to a lotus plant, then Śrutis are its roots, Śmṛtis are its stems and leaves, earlier Āḷvārs and acāryas are its nourishment, and Rāmānuja is that brightSun-light that caused the lotus flower to fully bloom.
>
> — ***Koti Sreekrishna***

Introduction

Śrī Rāmānuja (1017-1137) is regarded as one of the most systematic exponents of Viśiṣṭādvaita tradition. His *magnum opus Śrī Bhāṣya* is a living testimony to this fact. Śrī Rāmānuja gave a completely different orientation to the understanding of the quintessence of the *Upaniṣads*. He has both intellectual and social followers. Like Advaita, Viśiṣṭādvaita is also one of the oldest Vedāntic traditions. However, he is not the founder of this school. The other notable Viśiṣṭādvaitins are Yādava Prakāśa, Yāmuna, Periya Nambi, Goṣṭhipūrṇa. The fundamental tenets of Viśiṣṭādvaita are diametrically opposed to those of Advaita. The qualified non-dualism of Śrī Rāmānuja intends to preserve the identity of Brahman and the difference between *ātman* and Brahman, and also between *jīva* and God.[1] In his seminal work *Śrī Bhāṣya,* Śrī Rāmānuja equates Brahman, the supreme Reality, with Lord Viṣṇu. Like Advaita, Viśiṣṭādvaita too accepts *prasthānatraya* (the *Upaniṣads*, the *Brahma-sūtra,* and *the Bhagavadgītā).* In addition to these sources it also accepts *Pāñcarātrāgama.* Śaṅkara rejects these *āgamas* as non-Vedic. This could be seen as a major point of departure for Śrī Rāmānuja from Śaṅkara. Let us examine the fundamental difference between these two schools, namely, Adviata and Viśiṣṭādvaita.[2]

Metaphysics

Śrī Rāmānuja accepts the *Upaniṣadic* interpretation, like Śaṅkara, that Brahman is the ultimate Reality. But for Śaṅkara, Brahman is *nirguṇa.* According to Śrī Rāmānuja, Brahman is the unity of the differences constituting the world of our empirical experience; and is necessarily *saguṇa.*[3] According to Śrī Rāmānuja: "There is no knowledge of anything except through its attributes is possible."[4] In other words, Śrī Rāmānuja's Brahman is identity-in-difference (*bhedābheda*). Śrī Rāmānuja argues that pure identity as viewed by Śaṅkara is an abstraction, and it would be pure nothing. Logically speaking, the question of identity arises only when there is also difference. Of course, there are conflicting responses to this view from the scholars of Vedānta tradition. Satishchandra Chatterjee and Dhirendramohan Datta have their own reservations concerning the label attached to Śrī Rāmānuja's philosophy as *bhedābhedavāda.* On the one hand, Śrī Rāmānuja attacks Śaṅkara for showing identity relation between Brahman/Ātman as *tādātmya.* On the other hand, he shows the non-difference (*ananyatva*) between the world, including the *jīvas,* from its source (cause), the supreme Reality (Brahman).[5] Thus one finds contradiction in the position of Śrī Rāmānuja. But the same authors justify Śrī Rāmānuja's *bhedābheda* by citing an important *sūtra* (2.3.42) from the *Śrī Bhāṣya.* The self is both different and non-different from Brahman (God). On one account, self being imperfect it cannot be identical with Brahman (God), which is perfect. Thus one sees difference between the two. On the other account, Brahman (God) is inner substance of self (*ātman*). Apparently the contradiction vanishes as one can see both difference and non-difference between Brahman (God) and self (*ātman*).[6]

Further, Śrī Rāmānuja argues that there cannot be pure identity for it is an abstraction. Identity presupposes difference just as the latter presupposes the former. Śrī Rāmānuja finds justification in some rare *Upaniṣadic* passages to show the relation between Brahman, the self (*cit*), and the world (*acit*). The analytical texts clearly indicate that Brahman is the absolute Reality, self is the experiencing conscious subject (*cit*), and the material world is the non-sentient matter (*acit*).[7] There are also passages in the *Upanișads* that hold Brahman is the inner self (*ātman*) of all the entities. They constitute the body of Brahman. This is called body-spirit relationship (*dehātmasambandha*). It is mentioned in the *Bṛhadāraṇyaka Upanișad*: "He who dwells in the earth and within the earth, whom the earth does not know, whose body earth is, and who rules the earth within, he is the Self, the ruler within, the immortal."[8] These are the *ghaṭaka* or mediating texts. Further it is mentioned in the *Chāndogya Upanișad* that there a unity of Brahman with the world in its causal and effected aspect.[9] Śrī Rāmānuja takes all these three passages together to show that there are three ultimate existences constituting the Absolute: the eternal, omniscient, omnipotent God, the eternal but powerless soul, and the eternal matter. To be consistent with these analytical and mediating texts it is interpreted that Brahman is the unity of different selves and material objects of the phenomenal world. The analytical texts clearly distinguish Brahman from the selves (*cit*), and the material world (*acit*). Their intention is to show the transcendent nature of Brahman. The *ghaṭaka* or mediating texts indicate that Brahman is the inner self of all the entities. In other words, neither individual selves nor the material world can exist independent of Brahman. They form the body (*śarīra*) of Brahman. These texts also highlight the duality between Brahman as self, *cit* and *acit* as its body. They are otherwise known as the attributes of Brahman. The third set of texts uphold the non-dual nature of Brahman (God) as the supreme Reality. Both *cit* and *acit* enjoy their reality as the attributes of Brahman, which is the absolute reality. If the different passages occurring in the *Upanișads* are interpreted in this way one does not find any contradiction, according to Śrī Rāmānuja. In fact one can derive three different versions of thought from the above mentioned passages. There is unity when we observe Brahman as spirt, and its attributes (*cit* and *acit*) as its body. There is plurality when we observe individual souls and the world of material objects. There are both unity and plurality when we observe *abheda* and *bheda*. To quote from *Vedārthasamgraha*:[10]

> We uphold unity because Brahman alone exists with all other entities as his modes. We uphold both unity and plurality, as the

one Brahman himself has all the physical and spiritual entities as his modes and thus exists qualified by a plurality. We uphold plurality as the three entities — the individual selves, the world and the supreme Lord — are mutually distinct in their substantive nature and attributes and there is no mutual transposition of their characteristics.

In fact, the categorization of reality for Śrī Rāmānuja is based on substance (*viśeṣadravya*), and attribute or quality (*viseṣaṇa* or *guṇa*). It amounts to saying that everything in this world is either reduced to a substance or to an attribute. It is also possible that what is treated as substance from point of view can also be treated as an attribute from another point of view and vice-versa. Brahman is the substratum of these constituents. Strictly speaking, Śrī Rāmānuja's concept of unity is not unity but only a union. From a logical point of view, it is only a union of ultimately distinct and separate parts. This is clear from Śrī Rāmānuja's threefold categorical distinctions: the support (*adhāra),* the supported (*adheya),* the controller (*niyāmaka*), the controlled (*niyamya*), and the Lord (*śeṣin*), and the servant (the *śeṣa*).[11] *Ādhāra, niyāmaka, śeṣin* refer to Brahman (God), and *adheya*, *niyamya*, and *śeṣa* refer to the world (*acit*). In other words, for Śrī Rāmānuja, the distinction between Brahman and the world is very important and it cannot be dissolved. This view is further substantiated by Śrī Rāmānuja's statement that Brahman is related to world as the soul to the body.The soul of a person, although different from his/her body, controls and guides the body like a pilot in the ship. In the similar fashion, Brahman, although different from the world, controls and guides it as a ruler and controller.[12] To put it more succinctly, when we compare reality with a person, the plurality of selves and the world of objects constitute his/her body and Brahman is its soul. Apart from that, as attributes individual selves and the world of material objects are related to their substance, Brahman. The point that Śrī Rāmānuja drives home is that just as Brahman is real, its attributes the individual selves (*cit*), and the world of objects (*acit*) are also real, although they cannot be independently real. This is to say that individual selves and the world of objects are real qualities and modes of Brahman. Analogically speaking, individual selves and world of objects are related to Brahman as parts to a whole. Such an inseparable relationship is technically known as *aprathaksiddhi*. Each part is separate, yet not different in substance from the whole. Just as qualities are real but cannot exist independent of the substance of which they are qualities. Similarly, souls and objects are real as parts of ultimate reality but cannot exist independently of it. This is the reason that Śrī Rāmānuja's Absolute is not unqualified identity, but identity-in-difference. This made Śrī Rāmānuja's Vedānta, a qualified non-dualism. The world of phenomena is as real as Brahman and such a view is diametrically opposed to Śaṅkara's view, according to which the world of objects is only an appearance.

Epistemology

Coming to the theory of knowledge, Śrī Rāmānuja, unlike Śaṅkara, viewed that knowledge analytically implies the knower (subject) and the known (object). Therefore, it cannot be identified either with the knower or with the known. If there is no knower then there is no known too, for the knower and the known are interdependent. Śrī Rāmānuja argues that experience of reality is not an experience in which the distinction between self, and non-self is obliterated; but it is one in which the self becomes conscious of the unity of reality. The self remains distinct even in the experience of ultimate Reality (Brahman) just as the distinction between the knower and the known holds through and through in the experience of the empirical world.[13] Unlike Śaṅkara, Śrī Rāmānuja admits only three valid sources of knowledge. They are: perception (*pratyakṣa*), inference (*anumāna*), and verbal testimony (*śabda*). All other forms of knowledge are subsumed in one of these three forms. His views on indeterminate (*nirvikalapaka-pratyakṣa)* are also different from those of Nyāya and Advaita. When an object is perceived for the first time we do not know what it is. Such a perception is technically indeterminate. When the same object is perceived second time then we know what it is for we have come to know the identity of it. Śrī Rāmānuja's argument appears to be more logical for the object does not undergo the process of *nirvikalapaka-pratyakṣa* for the object is already experienced. We identify the animal as 'cow' for we have seen it before many times. Only in the first instance its identity is not known. When once its identity is known as such and such an object there is no *nirvikalapaka-pratyakṣa*.

Attributive Consciousness (*dharmabhūta-jñāna*)

The concept of attributive consciousness (*dharma-bhūta-jñāna)* is central to Śrī Rāmānuja's Viśiṣṭādvaita. A full blown explanation of this concept is found in the *Yatīndramatadīpikā* of Śrīnivāsācārya. An introductory work to Śrī Rāmānuja's Viśiṣṭādvaita.According to this view, consciousness directed towards the object is a quality (*dharma*) of the *ātman*.The acquisition of knowledge necessarily presupposes knower and known. For a knower there is something to be known out there, and what is known through a particular means of knowledge (*pramāṇa*) becomes knowledge. And the knower as subject is the bearer of this knowledge. But the prerequisite for a knower to be the subject, he or she possesses consciousness. In other words consciousness is attributed to the knower (subject). This subject can be called self (*ātman*) or empirical-I. To illustrate this point, one has to understand that one's perception of an object involves three components.[14] They are- myself as the conscious of the object (self), my consciousness of the object (consciousness of the embodied self), and the object of which I am conscious (the known). There cannot be just bare consciousness for "Consciousness cannot be aware of itself, but presupposes a self of which it is the idea or attribute."[15] It is always attributed to a subject (embodied self). Every knower possesses consciousness as his or her attribute. Therefore, it is appropriate to say that my consciousness of the object reveals itself to me, but not to itself. If it reveals itself to itself, it will be a person or ego or an 'I'. To claim that I know that I know the object is the same as saying that I know the object. Cognition and the cognition of that cognition are the same. For cognition is self-revealing. No other light is needed to reveal the presence of a light. Now, my 'I', as the knower, reveals itself to itself, but not to the consciousness revealing the object. Thus we have two forms of consciousness here. One that reveals itself to another and the other that reveals itself to itself only. The former belongs to the latter and it is its attribute (*dharma*). According to Śrī Rāmānuja, I-consciousness can never know itself without the role of attribute consciousness. And the attribute consciousness arises only when it reveals an object. Therefore, the "I" can know itself only when it knows an object. Further it must be noticed that Śrī Rāmānuja distinguishes between the consciousness that turned inward (*pratyak*) and that which is turned outward (*parāk*).[16]

These two are called existential and attributive forms of consciousness respectively. Not only that they are inseparable but also cannot work independent of each other. The existential consciousness, which knows itself, knows itself only when the attribute consciousness also works. In deep sleep attribute consciousness does not work for there is no object in that state. Since the attribute consciousness does not work in this state, even the existential consciousness does not know itself. Both these consciousnesses are eternal, but the existential consciousness is atomic in size (*aṇuparimāṇa*) for the *ātman* is atomic and the latter infinite. Although the attribute consciousness is infinite it has the power to contract and expand like a coil. When it contracts completely we do not know anything, if it contacts partially then we have finite knowledge. If it expands completely then we have infinite knowledge. The attributive consciousness is substance (*dravya*), although it is an attribute of *ātman*.[17]

The attributive consciousness also manifests in different states such as pleasure, pain, desire, hatred effort, and so on. For Śrī Rāmānuja, they are really the various forms of attributive consciousness operating through mind *(manas*). In a way, all the cognitive operations and consciousness experiences of individual self are the forms of attributive consciousness. The individual self (*ātman*) somehow gets identified with these experiences by involving itself in the various forms of Prakṛti, and its laws through its attributive consciousness.

As it is held by Śrī Rāmānuja, every entity has an identity, and its identity is known through the attributes that it possesses. Similar is the case with knowledge too. Knowledge at once is both a substance and attribute too. It is a substance insofar as it possesses the qualities of contraction and expansion. It is also viewed as an attribute for it is attributed to an individual self. In our normal classification substances are classified into spiritual (*cetana*) and material (*jada*). But Śrī Rāmānuja does not bring knowledge under either of these two categories and treats it as immaterial (*ajada*). It is not self-conscious and does not exist for itself, but exists only for the other (individual self).[18] The fundamental distinction between the self and knowledge, according to Śrī Rāmānuja, is the self is self-luminous and self-conscious too, but cannot reveal its object; whereas knowledge is self-luminous, but is not self-conscious. It reveals itself as well as its object.

This distinction between self and knowledge is very important in Śrī Rāmānuja's philosophy. The point that he intends to drive home here is that knowledge is always an attribute of self as an essential quality.[19] This is how Śrī Rāmānuja defends his concept of *dharmabhūta-jñāna.*

Śrī Rāmānuja's Critique of Śaṅkara's Doctrine of *Māyā/ Avidyā*

Śrī Rāmānuja advances seven arguments against Śaṅkara's *māyā* and *avidyā.* They are popularly called seven great untenables (*saptānupapatti*). They are as follows:[20]

1. *Āśrayānupapatti:* The nature of *māyā /avidyā* is ignorance or nescience. They are not two different things. The former is called cosmic illusion and the latter individual illusion. *Māyā* is basically understood in two different senses. In one sense, it is ignorance and in another sense it is the power (*śakti*) of Brahman by which the empirical world is manifested. According to Advaita, the two powers of *māyā* are— power of concealment *(āvaraṇa-śakti*) and power of projection (*vikṣepa-śakti*). Śrī Rāmānuja's first objection against *māyā/ avidyā* is: If ignorance (cosmic illusion) is what produces the world, then where does ignorance (cosmic illusion) exist? Certainly it cannot be said to exist in the *jīvā* for the *jīvā* itself is produced by ignorance being part of the created world. Therefore, it is absurd to say that effect produces the cause. Similarly, it cannot be said that ignorance exists in Brahman for otherwise Brahman cannot be omniscient.
2. *Tirodhānupapatti:*The second objection is that if ignorance is the veil that conceals the real nature of Brahman, then Brahman cannot be self-revealing power. Not only that *māyā/ avidyā* can veil or conceal Brahman only when it forgets itself. But it can forget itself only when it is concealed by *māyā* and *avidyā.* This is another vicious circle resulting in the fallacy of *circulus probando.*
3. *Svarūpānupapatti:*The third objection is that we cannot understand whether *māyā/avidyā* is positive or negative. If it is positive, it cannot be destroyed by knowledge as Advaitins

hold. Knowledge only recognizes the existence of the positive, but never destroys it. If it is negative it cannot combine itself with Brahman to produce the world. As negative, it is only absence of knowledge. But absence causes nothing. Therefore, to say that *māyā/avidyā* is both positive and negative is to uphold a self-contradictory position.

4. *Anirvacanīyatvānupapatti:* The fourth objection is that Śaṅkara's Advaita considers ignorance as neither real nor unreal nor both (*sadasatvilakṣaṇa).* This is an absurd locution for Śrī Rāmānuja. Such a locution violates the principle of non-contradiction for it is inexpressible. Something is real or unreal but it cannot be both and neither. It must be one of two. Such a position amounts to the violation of the law of excluded middle.
5. *Pramāṇānupapatti:*The fifth objection is that the presence of *māyā* cannot be established by any valid means of cognition. Ignorance is absence of knowledge and absence can never be perceived. To say that I perceive the absence of a rose on the table is as good as saying that I perceive the table, which exists as a positive entity. *Māyā* cannot be inferred for it lacks any peculiar characteristic. If it has any characteristic then it must be a real entity. But, according to Advaitins, it is not. It cannot be proved on the basis of scripture. According to the Veda, *māyā* is the mysterious power of Brahman. But for Advaitins Brahman has no characteristics hence it cannot have this mysterious power also.
6. *Nivartakānupapatti:*The Advaita interpretation of *avidyā* is such that it cannot be removed even by knowledge. What is this knowledge? It is the knowledge of Brahman that removes the ignorance which is responsible for the knowledge of the world. Now, does this knowledge of Brahman have Brahman as its object or is it the knowledge or consciousness that is the same as the Being of Brahman? According to Advaita, Brahman can never be the object of anyone's knowledge. It is same as one's *ātman*. Even the second alternative also does not remove the knowledge of the world, which is due to ignorance. The knowledge of myself does not remove the knowledge of the world. If Brahman is an object of my

knowledge, then world is also an object of my knowledge. Thus there are two kinds of objects and two cognitions. How can the knowledge of one can cancel the knowledge of other and show it to be the product of ignorance? Therefore, the knowledge of Brahman does not remove the knowledge of the world.

7. *Nivṛtyanupapatti:*Finally, if *avidyā* is a positive entity (*bhāvapadātha*), then its removal by knowledge is not possible. If ignorance means absence of knowledge of an object, then knowledge of that object removes that ignorance. If *avidyā* is a positive entity, then it cannot be removed by knowledge; but according to Advaita, *avidyā* is positive.

The above arguments advance by Śrĩ Rāmānuja clearly vindicate that the existence of *māyā/avidyā* is logically untenable. But Advaitins defend their position by saying that when it is said *māyā/avidyā* is indescribable, it means that an entity which is inexplicable cannot be described as real or unreal by this finite mind or intellect. But Śrĩ Rāmānuja considers *māyā/avidyā* as real and asks for its place and also a *pramāṇa* to know it. Echoing the views of Śrĩ Rāmānuja, Veṅkatanātha, also known as Vedāntadesika, in his *Śatadūṣani* saises the following objections. The most striking of them are: If Brahman is a homogenous entity without any qualification then the word 'Brahman' does not denote anything. If Brahman does not possess any qualities then it cannot be known for no enquiry into the nature of Brahman is possible. Then we have no right to talk about the knowledge of Brahman where it is not possible.[21]

God

Śrĩ Rāmānuja's Brahman, unlike Śaṅkara's, is *saguṇa* Brahman. He rejects Śaṅkara's distinction between *nirguṇa* and *saguṇa* aspects of Brahman. It is unity-in-difference and therefore contains within itself ultimate and indissoluble distinctions. The individual selves or souls and material objects of the world are related to Brahman as parts to whole. Brahman, in other words, is not qualityless, undifferentiated Pure Being but has real qualities. The three essential qualifications of *Brahman* are reality (*satyam),* consciousness (*jňānam*), and infinitude (*anantam*). Śrĩ Rāmānuja holds that Brahman (God) is the creator, sustainer and destroyer of the world God creates the world out of his own will. But creation does not mean that creation is out of nothing. Since the souls or selves and matter co-exist with God, creation means God's bringing about the world of variety and multiplicity which is potentially present in him. God wills Himself to be many and manifests Himself as many in the form of animate and inanimate entities. Apart from that, creation is not an event in time in the sense of having an absolute beginning in time. The world goes through the cycles of evolution (*śriṣṭi*) and dissolution (*pralaya*) as per the will of God, who is the Lord of *karma.*At the time of dissolution God withdraws world into himself. Even in the state of dissolution individual souls and matter remain distinct in Brahman, because individual souls (*cit*) and the world are eternal. According to Śrĩ Rāmānuja, the souls or selves are subtle (*sūkṣma)* and infinitesimal (atomic/*aṇuparimāṇa*), but eternal. The soul or self of Śrĩ Rāmānuja is not atman but only a *jĩvā* or empirical-I (the ego). At the time of creation God by his act of will manifests himself as selves and material objects. The kind of body that self receives depends upon its *karma.* However, God gives every self its freedom of will. Therefore, he is not responsible for the good or bad *karma* of the individual. Every soul or self acting out of will which God has graciously bestowed upon it is wholly responsible for its own state of existence. Consequently, Śrĩ Rāmānuja maintains that evil in the world cannot be traced to God, who is embodiment of all auspicious qualities or attributes that elevate him to the highest perfection.[22]

The above descriptions of God clearly show that for Śrĩ Rāmānuja there is no identity between God and soul or self.[23] According to him, the *Upaniṣadic* statement "That thou art" is radically different from that of Śaṅkara's. In Śrĩ Rāmānuja's case the 'that' here refers to God, the omniscient, omnibenevolent, omnipotent, infinite creator of the world. The 'thou' refers to God as existing in the form of man, the embodied self. Consequently Śrĩ Rāmānuja says that the identity between God and man is really the identity between God with certain qualifications and God with certain other qualifications. To put it in other words, God and man are of one substance but possess different qualities. Hence the name Viśiṣṭādvaita, the qualified identity, is the most suitable appellation for the Vedānta of Śrĩ Rāmānuja.

According to Śrĩ Rāmānuja, every judgment is a synthesis of distincts like subject and object that refer to the same entity. Suppose subject (S) and predicate (P) are absolutely distinct then the synthesis of the judgment 'S is P' will be a contradiction. If 'S and P' are absolutely identical, then it results in a tautology. There is no difference between pure difference and pure identity for both are abstractions. To put it succinctly, S and P refer to the same substance in two different forms. Śrī Rāmānuja's argument is that although the forms are different, they belong to the same organic whole. For instance, when we say 'The rose is red', the redness of the rose points to a complex red substance and the rose also points to a complex substance which has the quality of rose-ness. Therefore, the statement 'The rose is red' points to the identity of these two complexes. Here Śrī Rāmānuja reiterates that even God has His identity.He is both an inner self of the individual soul and God as the creator of the Universe are not different. The statement '*tat tvam asi'* has two components. The word 'tat' refers to the creator God and the word '*tvam*' refers to the God residing in the individual self *(jīva*). Therefore there is never a bare identity, but it is always qualified by some difference.

Liberation

Śrī Rāmānuja holds that the self's bondage to the body is due to its *karma*. This *karma* is produced and sustained by the self's ignorance of its own true being. Ignorance makes self believe that it is identical with body or with some part thereof and develops desires and attachments to bodily existence. The general tendency of the self is to identify itself with non-self makes it egoistic.[24] Liberation from ignorance, *karma* and bondage is to be attained through *karma, jñāna,* and *bhakti mārgas.* Every individual should perform the rites and ceremonies in accordance with his social duties (*varṇa-dharmas*) and station in life as enjoined by the Vedas. Therefore, the study of Mīmāmsā, whose objective is to suggest the right performance of rituals and duties, is essential for a Viśiṣṭādvaitin. Every individual interested in liberation must study the Vedāntic texts in order to know who he or she is apart from the nature of the world and God intellectually. As a result of study and reflection, man comes to know that in reality he is not identical with his body or any other material entity but a part of God himself, who is the creator, sustainer and destroyer of the universe. Individuals also realize that liberation cannot be attained either through the performance of rights and duties or by intellectual understanding alone, but only by free, loving grace of God. Therefore, the liberation seeking individual must devote himself or herself to the complete service of God. This is the reason why Śrī Rāmānuja regards *bhakti-yoga* as the path of liberation. It consists of meditation (*dhyāna),* prayer (*upāsana),* and devotion (*bhakti*). The spiritual aspirant must constantly remember God as his/her Lord and Savior. He or she should pray for God's mercy. The worshipper should completely surrender himself or herself to God for his her grace. Such complete self-surrender is called *prapatti.* It is only through this act of *prapatti* a worshipper is worthy of divine grace. Such a grace of God destroys ignorance, egoism, and *karma* of an individual to liberate him from bondage. The liberation, according to Śrī Rāmānuja, does not result in the effacement of the self or its uniqueness but resulb in eternal union with God. The liberated individual, instead of losing himself or herself in God, retains his or her individuality and consciousness and eternally enjoys the highest bliss in the infinite glory of God. Thus liberation, according to Śrī Rāmānuja, is not unity with God but eternal communion with God. Such liberation from bondage is possible only when the body falls off. Hence it is called *videhamukti.* The liberated soul enjoys perfect love and wisdom.

Concluding Remarks

Viśiṣṭādvaita is an important Vedāntic school after Advaita. It deviates from the fundamental precepts of Advaita by denying the notion of *nirguṇa* Brahman and the concept of *māyā*. Brahman is *saguṇātmaka.* This *saguṇa* Brahman is none other than Lord Viṣṇu. The individual souls (*cit)* and the world (*acit)* are Brahman's attributes. Just as Brahman is eternal, its attributes are also eternal although they are dependent on Brahman for their existence. The seven sound arguments advanced by Śrī Rāmānuja against *māyā/avidyā* of Advaita clearly indicate the logical tenor of his arguments. Similarly, one of the most original contributions of Śrī Rāmānujato Viśiṣṭādvaita is the concept of *dharmabhūta-jñāna.* The attributive consciousness being intentional in character is always directed towards an object and it is always attributed to a knower for consciousness by itself cannot be a knower. Coming to God (*saguṇa* Brahman), both *cit* and *acit* are His attributes. His identity is revealed through these attributes. On the one hand God is an indwelling spirit (*antaryāmin*) and on the other He is the creator. The ultimate goal of every soul is to attain liberation. The way to liberation is *bhakti* and *prapatti.* To get liberated from bondage one has to shed the body. Liberation "lies in being completely severing oneself from Prakṛti, when one takes on the body of the pure Transperant."[25] Such a view of liberation is technically known as *videhamukti.*

Notes

1. R. Puligandla, *Fundamentals of Indian Philosophy,* New Delhi:D.K. Printworld, p. 255.
2. P.T. Raju, *Structural Depths of Indian Thought,* New Delhi: South Asian Publishers, p. 439.
3. *Śrī Bhāṣya*, trans. George Thibaut: Oxford: Clarendon Press, 1904, p. 543.
4. P.T. Raju, *Structural Depths of Indian Thought,* p. 430.
5. S.C. Chatterjee & D.M. Datta, *An Introduction to Indian Philosophy,* Calcutta: University of Calcutta Press, 1984, pp. 421-22.
6. *Ibid.,* p. 422.
7. *Śvetāsvatara Upaniṣad,* I, 9-10 & IV, 9-10.
8. *Bṛhadāraṇyaka Upaniṣad*, 3, vii, 3-23.
9. *Chāndogya Upaniṣad*, VI, 2-8.
10. *Vedārthasamgraha*, Para.117.
11. *Śrī Bhāṣya*, II, I, 9.
12. *Ibid.,* II, ii, 3.
13. R. Puligandla, *Fundamentals of Indian Philosophy*, pp. 260-61.
14. P.T. Raju, *Structural Depths of Indian Thought*, p. 446.
15. P.N. Srinivasachari, *The Philosophy of Viśiṣṭādvaita*, Chennai: The Adyar Library & Research Centre, 1978, p. 27.
16. P.T. Raju, *Structural Depths of Indian Thought*, p. 446.
17. *Ibid.,* p. 447.
18. C.D.Sharma, *A Critical Survey of Indian Philosophy*, Delhi: Motilal Banarsidasss, 2016, p. 343.
19. *Ibid.,* p. 344.
20. P.T. Raju, *Structural Depths of Indian Thought*, pp. 450-5.
21. C. D. Sharma, *A Critical Survey of Indian Philosophy*, pp. 361-62.
22. R. Puligandla, *Fundamentals of Indian Philosophy*, pp. 264-65.
23. *Śrī Bhāṣya,* II, iii.45.
24. R. Puligandla, *Fundamentals of Indian Philosophy*, p. 266.
25. P.T. Raju, *Structural Depths of Indian Thought,* p. 454.

9

Some Indian Theories of Meaning

Introduction

The contribution of classical Indian philosophers to etymology, philology, and semantics is evident from the various theories of meaning advanced by them concerning words and sentences. Out of them two most popular ones are *abhihitānvayavāda*, *anvitābhidānavāda*. The former is advocated by Nyāya-Vaiśeṣika and Mīmāṁsā, and the later by Prābhākara Mīmāṁsā. Apart from these two the other two prominent theories are *apohavāda* of the Buddhists, and *sphoṭavāda* of Bhartṛhari. Perhaps a brief introduction of these theories may help us in understanding the complexity involved in understanding meanings of words and sentences. Language is the only medium through which dissemination of knowledge takes place in this empirical world. The kernel of any linguistic exercise is the semantic content of an expression or a sentence or a statement. A sentence is written but cannot be articulated, and a statement is articulated but cannot be written. A sentence is meaningful or meaningless by virtue of its syntactical structure. A statement is true or false by virtue of what it refers to. All our empirical transactions come to standstill when language goes on holiday, as aptly held by later Wittgenstein. There are debates among the philosophers of language concerning word-meaning and sentential meaning. Some hold that sentential meaning is dependent on word-meaning, and others hold that word- meaning is dependent on sentential meaning. An attempt is made in this essay to show the significance of Indian theories of meaning and their contribution to philosophy of language in general.

Abhihitānvayavāda

Nyāya-Vaiśeṣika, Bhaṭṭa Mīmāṁsā, and Vedānta subscribed to this theory of meaning. There are words (*padas*) with which we construct sentences (*vākyas*) with proper syntactical arrangement. Without words there are no sentences. Therefore, words become the primary units of our language. In order to understand the meaning of a sentence, first of all, we need to understand the meanings of its constituent words. When a word is uttered we make physical sound; and a sentence is a sequence of such sounds when it is articulated in the form of a statement. Sound is an intangible, yet perceptible physical phenomenon that is attributed to an all pervading substance called ether *(ākāśa).*Further, this sound is classified into *dhvani* and *varṇa.* The former is produced by any object, like a bell or drum, and is inarticulate, and the latter is produced by the action of the vocal organ of human beings. *Dhvani* is a mass of sound without any definite order or sequence. It is also held that a *varṇa* is a fixed character and has a definite place in the alphabets of any language.Without *varṇas* there is no human speech, for they exist both in written and spoken forms.[1] The written form of these *varṇas* is captured by visual sensation and the spoken form by auditory one. However, the sounds made by the animals and even by new born babies do not come under the category of *varṇa.* At the most they are brought under the category of *dhvani.*

A word is a group of *varṇas* or letters fixed in a definite order. This order cannot be changed, for any change of this sequence may result in a new meaning or no meaning at all. For instance, the word 'man' is arrive at by grouping the letters or syllables'm-a-n' in a given order. By changing their order we destroy the word itself. Similarly, the words 'won' and 'own' have same letters or syllables, but with different orders. By changing their order we get different meanings. Although both the letters or syllables, and words produce sounds, the sound of a word is a higher order one. When a word is uttered, the letters or syllables with which a word is constructed do not maintain their individual sounds. Even the words, like letters or syllables, have both spoken and written forms. Another significant distinction between a letter or syllable, and a word is that we cannot derive any semantic content from the former and but we do derive from the latter. This is the reason why Naiyāyikas hold: 'The essential nature of a word lies in its meaning. Logically a word is a sound that bears a certain meaning. The meaning of a word consists in its relation to the object which it signifies. A word may have different meanings according to the different ways in which it is related to any object."[2] This statement of Naiyāyikas clarifies that every word has a referent and the meaning of any word is dependent upon the object that it signifies or refers to. It is also held that the meaning of any word is not fixed for a word may change its meaning depending upon its relation to the object that it refers to. As P.T. Raju puts it, there are, at least, eight different ways of grasping the meaning of a word. They are as follows:[3]

1. from the grammatical point of view by knowing the subject of a sentence as per the rules of declension, and the place of noun in the sentence,
2. from the similarity of objects or referents in question (for example, a buffalo is like a bison),
3. from a dictionary (lexicon),
4. from the information given by a trustworthy person (*āpta*),
5. from our day-to-day social practice (*vyāvahāra*), like Swachh Bharat,
6. from the sentence in which the word occurs in a particular context, when we hear,
7. from the explanations (glossaries) of difficult terms,
8. from nearness to a significant word, as when we say that there is no room for religion in his philosophy, we understand that it is not the physical room but there is no scope for it in his philosophy.

Naiyāyikas hold that a word (*pada*) is a universal (*jāti*), structure (*samsthāna*), and individual. The structure goes both with the universal and the individual. For Mīmāṁsākas a word represents universal (*jāti*). The defense of Naiyāyikas is that when a person is asked to bring the cow he will bring the individual cow for he understands that the word 'cow' here refers to an individual cow characterized by a particular structure and universality (cow-ness). According to Nyāya, the child first leans the meanings of the words from 4 & 5. Such a view is also found in the writings of St. Augustine in his *Confessions,* and in early Wittgenstein's *Tractatus.* Children watch their elders and pick up the meanings of certain words through ostensive definition. For instance, the children are shown the charts of colours, fruits, animals, birds and so on, to identify them. Similarly, when the elders ask someone to 'bring a glass of water', the child observes and understands what it really means to 'bring a glass of water'. Thus Naiyāyikas uphold the doctrine of the relation of the meanings of the uttered words.

However, one can always doubt whether knowledge obtained through word-meaning is as authentic as the knowledge obtained through one's perceptions and inference. Someone would say 'There was a massive earthquake in 1947 that destroyed part of the earth in South Asia'. We can understand (cognize) the meanings of the words and understand what he says. But, we are skeptical about the truth of this utterance. It is in this context we look for validity of verbal knowledge.[4] The argument of Naiyāyikas is that if these words are the words of a trustworthy person, who is interested in the welfare of us, then they are true. When we teach language to children they trust in what we impart to them. The most trustworthy person among all is God, who composed the Vedas, according to Naiyāyikas. But, there are other trustworthy persons whose words are reliable to a great extent. It is not necessary that everyone knows everything. Sometimes we do not know the simple truths. We are ignorant of many things and happenings in our own life. We cannot accord same trustworthiness to the words in the conventional language as those of the words of the Vedas for the former are human creations. But there is also a trend where the words of the Vedas are often mixed up with those of conventional language in our popular discourse.[5]

Further, Naiyāyikas classify the words that derive their meanings from perceivable objects like trees, chairs and so on, and the words that derive their meanings form imperceptible objects like God, self, merit, demerit, and so on. The Vedas being trustworthy all our knowledge of imperceptible objects is validated by the Vedic authority. But in the case of perceptible objects we not only rely on God but also on other trustworthy persons who are interested in human welfare. Naiyāyikas hold that words are not mere sounds. These sounds produced by uttering the words have some power (*śakti*) and efficacy to mean objects. This does not mean that Naiyāyaikas accept power, force, efficacy, or energy as a separate category of reality. The inherent power or force or efficacy of a word is a quality. In fact, the power of a word to mean is God's desire. But later Naiyāyikas hold that some words being conventional their meanings are determined by their users. In general Naiyāyikas classify the word-meaning into the following four categories.[6]

1. The first is the meaning obtained from the word in question or from its parts directly (*yaugika*). The meaning of the word 'container' is obtained from the words 'contain' and 'er', and trailer ' from trail' and 'er' . There are many such words like 'cooker', 'school-master', and so on.
2. The second is the meaning not obtained from combining the meanings of the parts from the whole word (*rūdha*). For instance, the word 'shepherd' means one who guards or herds sheep. It neither refers to sheep nor to herd but to an individual who herds sheep.
3. The third is that in which the combined meanings of the parts coincide with the fixed meaning (*yogarūdha*). For instance, the word 'premier' refers to prime minister. As such 'premier' means the first. But here in this context he is the first among the ministers.
4. The fourth that in which a word have dual meanings. One meaning is derived from combining its parts, and the other is fixed independently in a particular sense. For example, the word 'Moravian' means a person who belongs to the nationality of Moravia. But now it is referred to a person who belongs to a particular Christian denomination of all parts of the world.

The types of meaning mentioned above are literal meanings assigned to the words. But there are also unexpressed and intentional meanings (*lakşanas*) of words. For instance, 'The village on the river', 'He fought like a lion in the war' have words like 'on' and 'lion' in the above sentences. A village cannot be situated on the river, but can be understood that the village is on the banks of a river. Similarly, a person's ability to fight in the war is compared with that of a lion.

In these cases we have to take only their intended meanings but not their literal meanings. But every word that we use does not have an intended sense or meaning. We need to be circumspect enough to convey the intended meaning for it is not completely divorced from its literal meaning. Lion is a courageous and fearless animal, we compare an individual with a lion only to show that he is as brave as lion. We do not compare a brave person with a jackal, which is known for its cowardice. Therefore, even the intended meaning is also somehow connected to it is literal meaning. Similarly, since a village cannot exist on a river, it is understood that it is at or by the side of a river. Hence, intendedness *(lakṣaṇa)* is defined as a relation of the word to a meaning which is itself is related to the literal meaning of the word.[7]

As already explained, a sentence is a group of words with a proper syntactical formation. A word is a combination of alphabets or syllables, and has its own meaning independent of the sentence in which it occurs. In fact, the sentential meaning is dependent on the words with which it is syntactically composed of. Naiyāyikas stipulate four conditions for sentential meaning. They are: *ākāṅkṣa, yogyata, sannidhi,* and *tātparya.*[8] Each of these conditions contribute to the word meaning, according to Naiyāyikas.

Ākāṅkṣa is known as expectancy. According to this condition, a sentence being a syntactically arranged combination of words there must be mutual expectancy from one another. No single word can convey meaning for the entire sentence. There are other words too in a sentence. Therefore, the words occurring in a sentence need to have relation with one another to meaning something collectively. In fact, the *ākāṅkṣa* or the expectancy of the words shows the relation between *kriyātva* and *kārakatva,* the verb and the case-endings implied by it.[9] When someone randomly utters the words like 'cow', 'dog', 'crow', etc., they do not mean anything collectively to form a sentence. This is because there is no relation established between *kriyātva* and *kārakatva* here in the strict grammatical sense. Even in the case of one's identity "so 'yam Srinivas", although there is no need for any relation between *kriyātva* and *kārakatva;* yet there is an expectancy of the words in the identity statement. When someone says that 'This is that Srinivas', in this statement both 'this' and 'that' have mutual implication for the identity of a person. Still further, when someone asks for a glass of water by uttering 'Bring me a glass of water', we tend to ask hot or cold. This is the significance of expectancy.

Yogyata is another condition which insists on the mutual fitness of the words within a given sentence. The words occurring within a sentence should not contradict each other. When someone says 'The fire is cool', then one does not see the mutual fitness of the words 'fire' and 'cool', for there is an apparent contradiction between these two words. The incompatibility between the meanings of the words in a sentence make a sentence totally meaningless. Of course, Navya Nyāya does not subscribe to this condition for we do not understand a sentence because we possess the knowledge of incompatibility of words through verbal cognition.[10]

The third condition *sannidhi* or *āsatti* expects proximity between the words of a sentence. A sentence to be meaningful it must contain words exiting contiguously so that one can establish connection among them. This is typically the case with written words. But, with long pauses one cannot expect contiguity among the spoken words. Hence, they cannot form a sentence. The long intervals of space between written words too does not make a sentence.[11]

The fourth condition *tātparya* brings out the intended semantic content of a given sentence. One word may have different meanings in different occurrences in different sentences. It is the intention of the person who used that word in a particular context (*prakaraṇa*) determines its meaning. It is the prerogative of the speaker or writer to use a word in its intended sense in particular context. Therefore, *tātparya* or intended meaning of a word is decided by the context in which it is used. When someone is looking for a person and asked about his whereabouts, it is replied by his associates 'He has gone to the bank'. Suppose his house is located on the bank of a river and also there is a commercial bank next to his house, there arises an ambiguity. To make it more clear his associates must say that he has gone to the bank to deposit some money. Therefore to derive the intended meaning of the Vedas, one has to strictly follow the logical rules of interpretation as advance by Mīmāṁsā.[12]

Well, we also find differences among the Indian philosophers of language concerning the importance given to *tātparya.* For some it is an essential prerequisite for verbal knowledge (*śabda*), and for others it becomes important only when it is struck by equivocation due to ambiguous expressions present in the sentence. There are also philosophers who hold that *tātparya* being a necessary condition for verbal knowledge (*śabda*), it cannot be treated as a separate condition by itself but can be part of *ākāṅkṣa*.But Vedāntins do not agree with this view as they believe that intended meaning is not a precondition for verbal testimony.[13] The contention of Vedāntins is that we may utter many expressions without any intention, yet others know their meanings. It is through the fitness of the words we derive a particular meaning. The fundamental difference between Naiyāyikas and Vedāntins is that the former claim that meaning is imported into the words through the intention of the speaker who uses them; while the latter hold that words have inherent primary meanings (*śakyārtha*). For instance, when new words are introduced into vocabulary we do use them with their primary meanings. A word cannot be introduced without any meaning. But Naiyāyikas counter this argument by holding that words do not always operate with their primary meanings, for we often talk about intended meaning of the speaker. The intended meaning of the speaker may not be the primary meaning attached to the word in question. Therefore, we need to accept that both primary meaning and intended meaning operate when we interpret any text. We have to take the appropriate meaning to serve the purpose.

Anvitābhidānavāda

Unlike Naiyāyikas, Bhāṭṭa Mīmāṁsākas, and Vedāntins, Prabhākara Mīmāṁsā advances a theory of meaning, according to which words refer to objects. Although the sounds produced by uttering the words are perceived through the sense of hearing, yet the objects referred to by the words are cognizable directly. For Prabhākara Mīmāṁsā words are nothing but meaning objects. He also makes it very clear that our cognition of the individual is due to the fact that individual essentially resides in the universal. One cannot think of universal without bringing it into the existence of the individual. Every sentence that expresses the commands is primary and "the meaning of no word can be understood without being associated with action."[14] For example, the command 'Open the door' makes a child first understand the meaning of the word 'door'. Further Prabhākara distinguishes between those words which are directly experienced or heard as commands and the words that are remembered.[15] The meaning of the former is understood only by associating them with an action; and the latter can be understood through the universals that they mean. Of course, the word whose meaning is understood through recollection should have also been understood through action, the noun, and the verb for their meanings are already related in a sentence. Therefore, the contention of Prabhākara is that there is no word with an independent meaning without being associated with an action; and a word cannot have its meaning a part from other words, especially with the verb of sentence. In other words, sentential meaning alone is the only unit of meaning. In a sentence the words are already related to each other through their meanings.

But Kumārila objects to Prabhākara's view. According to him, nouns even without being related to any actions have meanings. The child learns from the elders when a cow is pointed out and said 'This is a cow'. There are several sentences whose meanings do not prompt any actions. Some sentences are mere categorical type and they simply express what is (*siddhārtha*), and others express what is to be done (*vidhyartha*). Words, therefore, have their independent meanings, according to Kumārila. But when they occur in a sentence their meanings are combined together to arrive at sentential meaning. Hence, it is a misconception to think that words derive their meanings from their occurrence in the sentence.[16] In fact, the view of Prabhākara is closer to Nirukta view, according to which the meaning of a noun is dependent on verb (action). A noun is a mere modality of action. For Kumārila, meanings of nouns are not dependent on meanings of verbs (actions). It is evident that there exist doctrinal differences between Kumārila and Prabhākara concerning the theory of meaning.

Apohavāda

The doctrine of *apoha* is diametrically opposed to the above mentioned realist theories of meaning as a doctrine of exclusion. Both *abhihitānvayavāda* and *anvitābhidānavāda* hold that words refer to objects. But the Buddhist logicians like Digňāga, Dharmakīrti do not accept this view. According to them, the essence of meaning of words is negative and words are mere conceptual constructions of mind *(vikalpas*). Therefore, there is no connection between the words and external objects. A word being a conceptual construct of mind its essence is a negation of all its counter-correlates (*anyāpoha*). For instance, the word 'cow' is not really an animal with a snout, horns, dewlap, and so on. Rather it excludes all other objects that are not a cow.[17] Apart from that the Buddhists do not admit the reality of a positive entity called universal (*sāmānya* or *jāti*). For them only particulars (*svalakṣaṇa*) alone are real. This view of Buddhists is has direct bearing on their ontological position, according to which everything is under constant change. The doctrine of momentariness does not allow Buddhists to admit any permanent reality. According to Dharmakīrti, "the sensation of sameness is produced by a repeated series of the same perception, and that the sameness of the particulars is the consequence of the fact that they produce the same sensation."[18] Because of this rapid succession of these sensations we fail to notice the relative differences among them. Therefore, we tend to treat them alike in their nature. But the efficacy of the particulars is the basis of differentiation. Everything that produces certain results is different from that which does not produce them.

It is a known fact that the Buddhists do not admit *savikalapka-pratyakṣa* as pure form of perception. Any particular that is directly given to sense-experience is the real unerring knowledge of that particular. Therefore, it is the *nirvikalpaka-pratyakṣa* that is pure and unadulterated. But those who subscribe to *savikalapka-pratyakṣa* as a valid means of cognition, like Naiyāyikas and Mīmāṁsākas, hold that knowledge is not possible without conceptual transformation of our percepts. But for Buddhists the conceptual image of any object has not direct reference to the object in question. But the conceptual images have some impact on real life for we experience our own images and there is some sort of agreement among the images of different individuals. The doctrine of *apoha* clearly states that a word cannot signify a unique particular, for particulars are momentary. The difficulty here is that the verbal relation between a word and all the particulars that it refers to is not possible for these particulars belong to the past, present and future.[19] It is Digňāga in his *Pramāṇasamuccaya* explained the negative essence of the meaning. It is the most original contribution of him to the field of semantics. Digñāga clearly states that verbal cognition (*śabda)* is nothing but a form of inference (*anumāna)*. This identity he arrived at is based on their similarity of function on the basis of the principle of *anyāpoha*. But there is a need to know what the word '*anya'* stands for in *anyāpoha*. Digñāga recognizes a hierarchy of words in order to explain his positon. For example, synonyms (*paryāyaśabda*) do not exclude each other. The words '*vṛkṣa*' and '*taru*' are synonyms. They do not exclude each other's meaning. By definition they share the same meaning. The word '*vṛkṣa'* does not exclude the meaning of the universal word (*sāmānyaśabda/ jātiśabda*), '*pārthiva*', that which is made of the earth element. In other words, tree is made of earth element. Therefore, tree and earth are not opposed to each other. In fact, the word 'tree' enables us to understand (*niścaya*) the meanings of the words such as earth, substance and existence. In the hierarchy, the universal word of lower order does not exclude the universal word of higher order. They rather encompass the meanings of the words of higher order. Thus one finds invariable relation between the universal words of lower order and the higher order. This can be treated as a rule number one. However, the universal words of higher order neither exclude not encompass the meanings of the universal words of the lower order. This can be treated as the rule number two. So in the above mentioned cases, there is no exclusion.

Further he maintains that there are two types of exclusion (*apoha)*- direct and indirect. For instance the word '*vṛkṣa*' directly excludes the meaning of the word '*ghaṭa*'. But both these words share the same universal '*pārthiva*' (being made of earth element). But one finds that the universal words made of the same order exclude each other. Therefore, the word 'tree' excludes the word 'pot'. It is also argued that the word '*vṛkṣa'* indirectly excludes the word '*āpya'* (that which is made of water element). Thus one finds progressive exclusion of meanings of other wordsto establish the meaning of a particular word. This view of Digñāga is further substantiated by Sāntarakṣita in his *Tattvasaṁgraha.* There is no positive import of words. The following arguments would help us in understanding the negative essence of meaning.[20]

1. To arrive at similarity between the things that are absolutely dissimilar can be shown only by common exclusion of their counter-correlates. For instance, the animals, cat, dog, cow,

horse are dissimilar, yet they cannot be brought under one class by taking them all as excluding something else like as non-lions. The word 'cow' can be used to mean different colours of cows through the negation of the non-cow. Therefore, he word 'cow' does not positively refer to a cow.

2. In order to alternately affirm or deny anything it is done through the nature of exclusion of its counter-correlate. For every word there is an element common to both existence and non-existence. For example, the word 'cow' can be connected with 'is' or 'is not'. If the meaning of the word is positive then it cannot be connected with 'is not'. Even it cannot be connected with 'is' since it becomes redundant or superfluous. Therefore, the cognition of the common element must be attributed to some source that is negative in nature and it must lie in the exclusion of all other things.
3. If the objects of determinate perception are not cognized directly through the exclusion of their counter-correlates, then a person may ride on a donkey instead of a horse as he would not differentiate a donkey from a horse.

Further, Digňāga extends this negative approach to meaning even for the compound expressions like 'blue lotus'. In this case the word 'blue' excludes all those lotuses that are not blue, and the word 'lotus' excludes all those blue objects that are not lotuses. Thus the theory of *apoha* is as a theory of exclusion. But this theory is subjected to many a criticism. Both Naiyāyikas and Mīmāṁsākas admit the existence of universals unlike Buddhists. The meaning of a particular can only be explained through a universal. Unless there is a positive entity in the form of a universal, it is difficult to explain a particular like 'white cow'. Suppose the expression 'cow' excludes all non-cows, it will also include cows that are black, brown and white too. Therefore, there is a need to have a universal which subsumes all the particulars of a given kind. But contemporary philosophers like Barlingay defend *apoha.* According to him, Naiyā-Vaiśeṣika philosophers Praśastapāda and Udayana have equated Buddhist concept of exclusion (*vyāvṛtti*) with the concept of difference (*bheda*).They did not properly expound the Buddhist position. We know that the empirical world consists of discrete particulars. Also, "if it is agreed that in the explanation of these particulars the concept of *jāti* through *sāmānya-lakṣaṇa* invariably comes then it follows when we have knowledge of each particular we not only have the knowledge of the particular alone but also have knowledge of some other particulars, …"[21] The point that Barlingay drives home here is that when we have knowledge of one particular we also indistinctly possess knowledge of other particulars. But in the progressive process of exclusion we omit all those particulars that are indistinct. Hence, the *apohavādins* are nominalists. For a nominalist, words do not directly refer to objects outside us rather they represent our own mental images. There are no abstract and universal concepts. What we call general ideas such as 'cow' are only names and verbal designations that refer to a collection of objects or a series of particular events. The Buddhist theory of *apoha* perfectly fits into this stream.

Sphoṭavāda

Sphoṭavāda is another interesting theory of meaning advocated by Bhartṛhari (6th century AD) in his *Vākyapadīya.* But it was Patañjali who introduced the word '*sphoṭa*' in his *Mahābhāṣya* as early as in 2nd century BC. The word means 'to blast or to spurt'. In the context of philosophy of language, it is understood the meaning of an expression is revealed like a blast. The meaning of an expression remains unaffected although the individual speakers produce sounds (*dhvani*-s) short or long. The grammarians like Bhartṛhari hold that "a word or a sentence is to be considered not as a concatenation made up of different sound units arranged in a particular order, but mainly as a single meaningful symbol."[22] It is clarified by W.M. Urban in his *Language and Reality* that the word 'symbol' is used in the sense of a linguistic sign. The words '*śabda*' and '*sphoṭa*' are central to Bhartṛhari's philosophy of language. The former stands for the universal or essential structure of language and the latter for meaning-bearing unit and necessarily a part of the former.

Language, according to Bhartṛhari, can be interpreted from its universal as well as from its particular sense. In its universal sense, language is the essence of all linguistic phenomena. In its particular sense, it represents particular languages that manifest the essence. All human languages are brought under the category of particular languages wherein sounds are produced to communicate something to the other for all these languages are temporal. Further these sounds are categorized into phonemes, words, and sentences. This is general structure of any particular language. The task of Bhartṛhari as a grammarian is to link these particular languages with the universal language (*śabda*). Of course, the relation between One and many is a metaphysical one. It is also true that one finds similarities between the approaches of Bhartṛhari and Advaita. However, it needs to be clarified here that Bhartṛhari as a grammarian is an independent thinker.

Bhartṛhari attempts to solve this issue of relation between One and many from a linguistic point of view by holding that particular languages are the various manifestations of one universal language called *śabda.* This is what Vedāntins called *Śabda Brahman.*To quote him in this context: "Just as a reflection formed elsewhere (i.e.. in water) appears, due to the activities of the water, to partake of the water, similar is the relationship between the word and the speech-sounds."[23] This imagery provides us with a clue that *sphoṭa* hidden in the *śabda* is reflected in the sounds uttered through speech. It also takes the form or shape of these sounds for communicating the semantic content (meaning) of the speech-sounds. The speech-sounds may vary from particular language to another, but their underlying *sphoṭa* or *śabda* is one and the same. Further Bhartṛhari maintains that: "The inner principle called 'speech' which exists egg-like, evolving into speech-activity, assumes sequence through it parts."[24] The linguistic essence manifests in many ways through multiple languages is the inner principle of all particular languages and speech-activities. This inner principle is technically called *sphoṭa.*

Sphoṭa as a meaning-bearing principle underlies the various speech-phenomena. As a metaphysical principle, *sphoṭa* is beyond the limitations of space-and time. In other words, it is one and indivisible. Further Bhartṛhari maintains that: "People talk of difference in diction (as belonging to the utterance) of the Word, which itself is the undivided time, but (appears to) follow the time-patterns of the speech-sounds (uttered), in accordance with the differences in the causes of its being perceived.[25] In essence, all of our day-to-day speech-acts are regulated by this metaphysical principle.

Well, our language involves time intervals. Our speech not only involves meaningful sounds but these sounds are uttered in different time intervals*(nāda)*. This is how speech becomes a temporal event. Also, it is through speech we assert the events of past, present, and future. Change is represented by time. It stands for the succession of events that take place in this empirical world. In this sense, time stands for the sequence of speech-sounds produced. Bhartṛhari meticulously distinguishes *dhvani* or *nāda* from *śabda*. The former is temporal and the latter is eternal. Although our natural languages are temporal their very essence is eternal. This is the central feature of Bhartṛhari's philosophy of language. Bhartṛhari claims that words have no traceable beginning. We do not really know whether they are created or eternal like human beings. The words are eternal.[26] Although the *śabda* is indivisible and eternal, the speech-activities make it appear to be temporal and ever changing. But it is other way round. The *śabda* as a timeless essence manifests itself through the temporality of linguistic activities. For Bhartṛhari, *śabda* being eternal temporality cannot be ascribed to it.

Further, it is noticed in the philosophy of language of Bhartṛhari that *śabda* is the ultimate reality and is the origin of all things in this empirical world. To quote him in this context: "That beginningless and endless One, the imperishable Brahman of which the essential nature is the Word, which manifests itself into objects and form which is the creation of the universe."[27] This ultimate reality is known as *śabda* Brahman. As a grammarian, Bhartṛhari is of the opinion that language is the source of this empirical world. All the objects of the world are located in spatio-temporal matrix, but *śabda* alone is trans-empirical and immutable. Therefore, the source of worldy existence is attributed to "which, Single One, the cause of all, belongs this manifold existence, under the forms of the enjoyer, the enjoyed and the enjoyment."[28] The *śabda* has creative potency and the objects of the empirical world are dependent on language for their existence. Every object exists in language in its embryonic form. It is through the power or potency of the *śabda* which is the creative energy, an object gets manifested. This creative energy is called *sphoṭa,* the word power. According to Bhartṛhari: "Now, in reality, can there be a preceeding and subsequent part in timeless entities? This appearance (of sequence) is the result of the powers inherent in the integral entity itself."[29] The underlying power within the language or in the word multiplies itself into parts so that its manifestations are many although the language-principle is One and immutable. This is how the world springs form the Word (*śabda*).

From the above analysis it follows that the objects in the world cannot have reality of their own for they arise out of the language. If at all they have any reality their reality is empirically valid. But at the absolute or trans-empirical level they are just the projections of the language. At the trans-empirical level the world of objects is embedded in the language. To quote Bhartṛhari in this context: "Those who are versed in the Vedas know that this Universe is the transformation of speech. It was out of the Vedas that the Universe was first evolved."[30] Insofar as the language and the world are concerned both share same logical form, to put it in the language of early Wittgenstein, for they are one and the same. Further Bhartṛhari classifies language into *para, paṣyanti, mādhyama and vaikhāri.*[31] Each of these represents a stage in which language is located. The ultimate stage of language is known as *para vāk,* a stage below that is *paṣyanti,* where we find the identity of thought and language.[32] The middle stage is called *mādhyama* and the gross empirical linguistic acts belong to *vaikhāri vāk.*This division makes us realize that language become more and more subtler and refined when it moves from gross level to the level of *para vāk.* The day-to-day language consists of speech-acts of different sorts and are located in space and time. As such language is One single reality and is indivisible. Bhartṛhari further clarifies: "The Word is neither a 'previous' nor 'a subsequent', because it is the speech-sounds which are produced in sequence. But the non-sequential is revealed as sequential as if it were divided."[33] Hence, what is sequential is produced from non-sequential. What is timeless appears to be temporal. What is timeless is transcendental. This is the Beyond, and it needs to be investigated further. This absolute and timeless language mentioned earlier is the source of everything. The plurality of languages which we speak at the empirical level are rooted in the absolute and timeless language. The sounds, word–patterns, and sentences we have in individual languages are unified by one single principle called *sphoṭa.*

Further Bhartṛhari holds that *śabda or sphoṭa* is in the mind and is of the nature of a thought. But thought expresses itself in the form of language. It cannot exist independent of language. In a way thought and language are identical. The following analogy of Bhartṛhari may help us in understanding this identity. As he writes: "Just as the light which is in the fire-stick acts as the cause for further lights, similarly the Word which is in the mind is the cause of the speech-sounds."[34] As a grammarian he holds that all consciousness is permeated by language. Our conscious acts are expressed in language and our acts become intelligible only through language. Of course, it is very clear from the arguments of Bhartṛhari that language as universal principle is primary and mind is secondary. It can be treated as a kind of instrument though which language operates. Again, as a grammarian, Bhartṛhari highlights the significance of grammar for it provides a structure to language both in its universal and particular aspects. Not only grammar regulates our language but also purifies mind and soul. To quote Bhratṛhari in this context: "The wise say that grammar, nearest to that Brahman and the foremost spiritual training is the most important (of such) subsidiary texts of the Veda."[35] It is the pure form of language leads us to Brahman.

Another significant contribution of Bhartṛhari to philosophy of language is his *akhanda* theory of meaning. According to this theory, just as language is eternal and its meaning as inner essence is also eternal. Thus meaning, like language, becomes transcendental. Concerning the sentences, Bhartṛhari writes: "Just as a single homogenous picture is described though various features as being blue (green, etc.) as a result of being perceived in different ways, similarly the sentence which is single and does not possess expectancy is described in terms of words which possess mutual expectancy."[36] A sentence cannot be divided into parts for it is a whole and its meaning is also holistic. The words which constitute a sentence are not independently meaningful and are also not independently real. Therefore, the word-meaning is completely dependent on sentential meaning. Therefore, Bhratṛhari's *akhanda* theory accords primacy to sentences over the words. To substantiate this view, writes Bhartṛhari: "The Word has no parts; how then can its meaning have any parts? The ignorant person gets a different idea of its formation by splitting it into parts."[37] Perhaps a person who does not know the genuine nature of language and grammar alone can resort to divide sentence into parts. A grammarian always looks for a unitary meaning which timelessly remains at the back of every linguistic unit.

Bhartṛhari vehemently criticizes both *abhihitānvayavāda* and *anvitābhidānavāda* on the ground that they arrive at the meaning only through a kind of composition of words. In nutshell, the words independent of sentences in which they occur have their own meanings. Hence, the sentential meaning is dependent on word-meaning. The division of language and its meaning into parts is not acceptable to Bhartṛhari. According to him: Now, in reality, can there be a preceding and subsequent part in timeless entities? This appearance of sequence is a result of the powers inherent in the integral entity itself.[38] Both Naiyāyikas and Mīmāṁsākas, excepting Prabhākara Mīmāṁsā, admit the independent word-meaning. Prabhākara argues that words do not have completely independent meaning for their meaning is often derived from their contextual use. The view of a grammarian is always different from a non-grammarian. Bhartṛhari being a grammarian views that language and its essence (meaning) are one and immutable. Therefore, the theory that parts make up a whole is not acceptable to him insofar as language is concerned.

Concluding Remarks

The philosophy of language in the Indian contextis both complex and complicated. The various theories of meaning advanced by the classical Indian philosophers suggest that the theory of meaning is approached from two different standpoints. They are: epistemological and metaphysical. By and large the approach taken by the Naiyāyikas, the Mīmāṁsākas, and the Buddhists can be brought under epistemological category and the approach of Bhartṛhari under metaphysical one. Further, Naiyāyaikas and Mīmāṁsākas are brought under the category of realism, and the Buddhists under anti-realism. The realists accept the view that words as concepts are real, and they refer to objects as their referents. Thus one can see a kind of correspondence between the words as concepts and the objects as their referents. Apart from that, words as concepts are treated as universals, and these universals participate in the particulars. This thesis may hold good for a realist. But the Buddhist nominalists do not subscribe to this position as they do not accept the reality of the words as concepts. For there are no universals, words are mere names and they refer to mental images (*vikalpas*). These mental images do not refer to anything directly but only help us in eliminating through negation or progressive exclusion of those particulars which a word designates. The word 'cow' as a particular acquires its meaning by excluding all 'non-cows'. As anti-realists and anti-essentialists, the Buddhist phenomenalists do not subscribe to anything that is permanent, for the phenomenal reality is an ever changing one. The explanation of Barlingay may help us understanding the position of the Buddhists. Let us imagine the world is occupied by the particulars *A, B, C, D, E.* To have the knowledge of *A* one has to progressively eliminate the indistinct knowledge of *B, C, D, E.* One finds mutual exclusion here. *A* excludes *B, C, D, E* and vice-versa. If one tries to understand the Buddhist theory of *apoha* in terms of difference or *atyantābhāva* then its very purpose is defeated. Coming to Bhartṛhari's *sphoṭavāda,* it rests on a metaphysical position which subscribes to strict monism and absolutism. Everything else is derived from this absolute first principle called *śabda* or *sphoṭa*. Meaning as the essence of language is as eternal as language and ultimately the supreme Reality is equated with language. What we encounter in our day-to-day world is many manifestations of this one single, indivisible language. The multiple languages derive their essence from one unitary principle *śabda* or *sphoṭa.* But the arguments of Bhartṛhari have their own logic. When the meaning of a sentence is revealed, it is revealed all at once like a blast. Sentential meaning is not a mere composition of the words with which it is made. When we conjoin the words by meticulously following the rules of syntax to form a sentence, the independent meanings of these words do not necessarily contribute to the sentential meaning. In fact the words derive their meanings because of their occurrence in a sentence dependent upon the context in which a sentence is used. As Aldous Huxley pointed, it is impossible to live without metaphysics; but the only choice left for us is to choose between the good or the bad one.

Notes

1. Satishchandra Chatterjee, *The Nyāya Theory of Knowledge*, Calutta: University of Culcutta Press, 1978, p. 323.
2. *Ibid.*, p. 324.
3. P.T. Raju, *Structural Depths of Indian Thought,* New Delhi: South Asian Publishers, 1985, p. 216.
4. *Ibid.*
5. *Ibid.*

6. *Ibid.,* p. 217.
7. *Ibid.*
8. Viswanatha Pancanana, *Bhāṣāpariccheda,* Bombay: Nirnaya Sagar Press, 1915, p. 82.
9. Satishchandra Chatterjee, *The Nyāya Theory of Knowledge*, p. 336.
10. *Ibid.,* p. 337
11. *Ibid.,* p. 338.
12. *Ibid.*
13. *Ibid.,* p. 339.
14. P.T. Raju, *Structural Depths of Indian Thought,* p. 48.
15. *Ibid.*
16. *Ibid.,* p. 49.
17. K. Kunjunni Raja, *Indian Theories of Meaning*, Chennai: The Adyar library & Research Centre, 1969, p. 79.
18. *Ibid.*
19. *Ibid.* pp. 81-2.
20. *Ibid.,* p. 83.
21. S.S. Barlingay, *Reunderstanding Indian Philosophy,* New Delhi: D.K. Printworld, 2014, p. 71.
22. K. Kunjunni Raja, *Indian Theories of Meaning*, p. 97.
23. Bhartṛhari, *Vākyapadīya: Critical Text of Canto I and II,* edited & translated by K. Raghavan Pillai, Delhi: Motilal Banarsidass, 1971, I, 49.
24. *Ibid.,* I, 51.
25. *Ibid.,* I, 75.
26. *Ibid.,* I, 28.
27. *Ibid.,* I, 1.
28. *Ibid.,* I, 4.
29. *Ibid.,* I, 22.
30. *Ibid.,* I, 120.
31. *Ibid.,* I, 143.
32. B.K. Matilal, *The Word and the world: India's Contribution to the Study of Language,* Oxford: OUP, 1990, Chapter.8.
33. Bhartṛhari, *Vākyapadīya: Critical Text of Canto I,* 48.
34. *Ibid.,* I, 46.
35. *Ibid.,* I, 11.
36. *Ibid.,* II, 8-9.
37. *Ibid.,* II, 13.
38. *Ibid.,* II, 22.

10

The Other in Indian Philosophy

Introduction

The notion of 'the other' is one of the most interesting subjects of inquiry in philosophy. All our references to 'self' presuppose that there is something called non-self. In one sense self is understood as something immutable and non-self refers to that which is transient and mutable. The former is known as *ātman* and the latter *anātman*. This distinction between *ātman* and *anātman* is precisely based on metaphysical considerations. But when it comes to epistemology, the self is the subject of and the other becomes the object. The epistemological self is nothing but empirical-I or *jīva,* which is a psycho-physical entity. This is also called transcendental subject by the philosophers like Kant and Husserl. There are multiple of them and each one of them performs the role of a subject as well as well as an object. As moral agents *jīvas* have obligations towards the other. Even our ordinary language is designed in such a way that 'I' presupposes 'he', 'she', and 'it'. In the absence of them, 'I' becomes totally meaningless for the empirical world is not a solipsistic one. Existentialism in the Indian context necessarily involves the other. The other is very significant for the purpose of debate, argument, and dialogue, and the very linguistic communication presupposes a hearer-speaker situation. Our family and social life is derived from the other.

In the West, the existentialists like Jean-Paul Sartre portrayed the other as hell. He derived the negative consequences of the other.

But in any egalitarian society the other becomes an important component. The solitude of an individual destroys his/her social life. But the defenders of Sartre would say that loneliness leads one to calmness of mind. If everyone wants freedom from the other, then what happens to the social life of an individual? Our *puruṣārthas—dhrama, artha, kāma,* and *mokṣa* remind us of our social responsibilities. All our social relations are completely dependent on the other. As Sri Aurobindo felt that it is unimaginable to think of a man without a society and vice-versa. A society does not consist of discrete and isolated individuals. The very existence of a society presupposes dynamic social relations among the citizens of society. Thus social life becomes a prerogative of a *jīva.* It is the social life of individuals that teaches them their responsibilities as obligations towards the other. An attempt is made in this essay to show the positive consequences of the other from the point of view of Indian philosophy.

Jīva as a Moral Agent

All of us as empirical beings (*jīvas*) act as moral agents. And each one of us is responsible for the moral actions that we perform. One cannot blame the other for one's actions for he/she has to reap the fruits of one's own actions. This is typically the essence of the law of *karma,* which is the central doctrine of Indian philosophy. And it is a truism that Indian philosophy is highly realistic wherein the ideals of life are embedded. Although the *Upaniṣads* reiterate that the reality is One and indefinable, we cannot ignore the plurality that we encounter in our day-to-day life. In the *ChāndogyaUpaniṣad* it is mentioned that: "In the beginning, my dear, this (world) was Being alone, one only, without a second (*ekamevamadvitīyam*)."[1] This Being is devoid of all qualities or attributes (*nirguṇa, nirviśeṣa, niravayava,* and*avyakta*) is unmanifest. Thus the *Upaniṣad* advocates strict monism (*kevalādvaita*). Further the *Upaniṣads* hold that: "All this verily (is) Brahman (*sarvamkhalidam Brahman*)."[2] and "this Ātman (is) Brahman (*ayamātma Brahman*)."[3] So we find an apparent contradiction in what the *Upaniṣads* and what we experience as ordinary empirical individuals. It is in this context the ingenuity of the philosophers like Śaṅkara comes to our rescue. Yes, both monism and pluralism exist as polar concepts. The phenomenal or pluralistic reality presupposes noumenal one. The former is known as *vyāvahārikasatta*, and the latter *pāramārthikasatta.* They are treated as two levels of reality. All our day-to-day experiences belong to the *vyāvahārika* level. Therefore, our analysis of the other necessarily rooted in this sphere of reality.

Often it is claimed by the critics that Indian philosophy is idealistic, self-centric, pessimistic, spiritual and other-worldly oriented. It only shows that people have not really gone into the structural depths of Indian philosophy. Indian philosophy catered to both social and spiritual needs of the individuals. How can anyone bypass the social to attain spiritual level? It is only at the social level an individual is trained to attain his/her spiritual heights through proper initiation by a teacher *(guru)*. It goes without saying that the survival of any philosophical tradition is dependent upon its social import, and social reality necessarily recognizes the presence of the other. Our language, logic, ethics, ideologies, interpersonal relations assume meaning only in the context of the other. Thus, the other has deep philosophical significance. No philosophy would ever advocate any ideology or profess anything without noticing the existence of the other. The 'I' or 'ego' or '*ahaṁkāra*' does not make sense in the absence of the other. I say that "I am an Indian" because there are also individuals belonging to other nations. The 'I' is one among the many. The 'I' always tries to distinguish itself from the other. The identity of an individual self *(jīva)* is purely dependent upon accidental qualities (*taṭasthalakṣaṇa*). The individual identity is a necessary prerequisite for individual as a moral agent. Thus the 'other-ness' persists in the world of plurality. Indian philosophy does not deny this fact. One who does not recognize the existence of the other is like a frog in the well. A frog thinks that the well is the universe and there exists nothing outside it. Although the *Upaniṣads* maintain that the supreme Reality is One, they gave due importance to the individual selves *(jīvas)* and the world of plurality.

The empirical world is the social nexus of individual selves, but the ultimate goal of every individual self is to attain the liberation (*mukti*) without neglecting one's own social responsibilities. The code of ethics prescribed by *Dharmaśāstras* has universal applicability. It is like Immanuel Kant's 'Categorical Imperative'. In this sense, no orthodox system of Indian origin has ever propagated solipsism. The essential nature of human beings is the same everywhere. The divisions among human beings on the basis of their external features are only artificial creations of the finite, immature human mind. But these divisions are taken very seriously as long as this empirical existence is concerned. What is accidental is taken as essential by the individual selves under the influence of ignorance (*avidyā*). Just as the prisoners in Plato's myth of the cave mistook the shadows on the walls of the cave as real, we the individual selves mistake this world of names and forms for the eternal world. The empirical world is real in its own right; but its reality cannot be compared with the reality of Brahman/Ātman, which is its ground. A shadow is the shadow of something. On its own a shadow cannot exist. Since we experience it is technically possesses objective existence, but it cannot be treated as real existence.

The Same Self in the Other

What is existentially real for an empirical individual is not real at the level absolute (*pāramārthika*) level. In the Indian context, philosophy and religion are promiscuously mixed up. Therefore, one does not find any tension between philosophy and theology. For example, Hinduism is both a way of life and a religion. The religious roots of Hinduism, and the philosophical roots of orthodox Indian philosophical systems are the same (the Vedas). The Self (Ātman) in man is the same as the one found in the lower creatures. It is mentioned in the *Upaniṣads,* "The essential self or the vital essence in man is the same as that in an ant, the same as that in a gnat, the same that in an elephant, the same as that in three worlds, indeed the same as that in the whole universe."[4] Behind the psycho-physical man is the Self, which is spiritual and divine. It is mentioned in the *Īśa Upaniṣad*:

> He who sees all beings in his own Self and his own Self in all being, has thereby, no more loathing (for the others). When to the knowing man all beings are but his own self, then for him who sees unity, what delusion is there and sorrow? The face of the Truth is hidden with a golden plate: that, O Sun, the nourishing Lord! remove, so that I may realize the Truth.[5]

It is possible for us to hate others when that awareness of unity is not there. In the *Bṛhadāraṇyaka Upaniṣad* there is an interesting dialogue between the sage Yājňavalkya, and his virtuous wife, Maitreyi. First of all, such a dialogue is possible only when there is the other who is competent enough to have a dialogue with one. In the ensuing dialogue

Yājñavalkya says that our awareness of the Self in all makes everyone dearer to us. The spiritual goal of Indian philosophy is to experience this divine Self (Brahman/Ātman) within and without.

But, as ordinary human beings, we refuse to recognize this sublime truth. We crave for those things that boost our sensuous pleasures. Therefore, the classical Indian ethics introduced the notion of '*dharma*', an overarching principle that regulates social life of the individuals. It is a backbone of society in the Indian context. *Dharma* literally means that which supports, that which holds together the peoples (of the Universe). It is not merely a set of beliefs having no necessary connection with the daily life of humanity, but a set of principles of healthy and beneficent life. *Dharma* resolves the conflict between the material and the spiritual, the temporal and the eternal. It recognizes that, while striving after the ideal one cannot afford to overlook the actual. It promotes a way of life which takes care of the material and spiritual sustenance and growth of both the individual and society. Therefore the other becomes important in the family and the society. There is no social life without the other. We rely on the other for our day-to-day life. Our language derives meaning only from the existence of the other. Thus the existence of the other is not only a truism but also a necessary condition for one's own existence.

Once we admit that we cannot dispense with the role of the other in our social life, it goes without saying that somehow all our social actions originate from the other. However, the other has two important dimensions, namely, positive and negative. In its positive aspect the other is one who shares one's happiness, feelings, and misery. The other in this sense is an embodiment of energy, forgiveness, endurance, purity, freedom from pride and hatred. This results in a mutual respect. Individuals make up a family. For the well-being of an individual, the familial relations among the members of a family have to sustain. The strong familial relations strengthen the social relationships for families make up a society. The principal objective of the classical Indian ethics is to bring about happiness by establishing harmonious relations among the people. The social duty (*samāja-dharma*) of an individual is to protect harmonious relations among the individuals for the furtherance of the humankind. There is a reference in the *Mahābhārata*, "Do unto others as you would they should do unto you."[6] This is what is echoed by Kant in his 'Categorical Imperative'. In its negative aspect, the other is one who aims at destruction of harmonious relations among the individuals that results in jarring wishes, friction between ourselves and the other, the lack of mutual support and mutual sympathy. In this sense, the other is an embodiment of hypocrisy, arrogance, conceit, wrath, harshness, and un-wisdom. In fact, these are qualities of a demon, according to Hinduism. The establishment of harmonious relations means the sacrifice of mutual selves. Courtesy and consideration for the feelings of the others are enjoined as general principles of conduct. Noble bearing and manners are considered to be the hallmark of an Aryan. It is not merely the sympathy towards the other, but empathy that makes our relationship with the other more secure and strong in any society.

Theodor Adorno explained the nature of dialectics that operates between the one and the other in his very important work *Negative Dialectics* (1966). According to him, dialectics operates in the process of socialization. But it is not the positive dialectics as viewed by Hegel and Marx. Positive dialectics escalates social tensions among the individuals and various social groups. This results in the destruction of social harmony among the individuals living in a society. But, Adorno claims, this is not the case with negative dialectics. It always tries to bring the other into the fold of process of socialization. There exists no obvious tension between humans and nature. If we look at the nature as the other responsible for our misery then nature looks at humans from a similar point of view for we indulge in the destruction of nature for our survival. But if we look at nature as our friend, then the other remains no more as the other. It becomes one with you. One can certainly draw parallels between the views expressed by Indian philosophers and Adorno. According to *Dharmaśāstras,* the natural superiors of humans are God, parents, teachers, and elderly. The other cannot claim his/her superiority over his/her fellow human beings, for the other is one among them. The other becomes dangerous or a threat to humanity only when he or she behaves like Nietzsche's superhuman. Although the classical Indian tradition propagates nonviolence (*ahimsā*), it does not by any means encourage cowardice. It is not blind to the fact for it is realistic. We must put up with one kind or another of violence to protect ourselves ad to safeguard the interests of the society in general. However, since the sense of tolerance has been given highest priority in the classical Indian ethics, there is a point when it loses its ground. If a nation attacks you without any provocation, it is unreasonable to expect you to be tolerant towards the aggressor when innocent people have lost their lives. The *Ārya-dharma* is to protect your kith and kin, and your people against the evils of unprovoked war. What the classical Indian ethics expects its followers to do is to conscientiously minimize violence as much as possible. It is mentioned in the *Bhagavad-gītā:* "He who does not have the sense of agency or egoism, whose intellect does not hold it responsible for action performed by the body and the senses, he does not kill, nor does he become bound by the result of such killing."[7] This is typically the view of a person who is enlightened. But we are dealing with the empirical individuals who are yet to get enlightened.

As aptly pointed out by Francis Bacon, "Knowledge is power." According to classical Indian philosophers, however, knowledge leads to spiritual power, but not to political power. The empirical knowledge of incidental sciences leads to control over nature, but the spiritual knowledge leads us to liberation from the bondage. Thus a spiritual aspirant looks for that power which releases him from bondage. One who possesses spiritual power alone is superhuman. He is powerful for he is enlightened. He is regarded as superhuman not because of his might over others, but because of his wisdom. When a superhuman is asked the question: Who are you? His answer would be that I am essentially same as you, but accidentally different from you. As a matter of fact, the Indian concept of renunciation is misunderstood and misinterpreted by most scholars. They take it for a negative virtue; therefore, it is seen to have no social value. But it is clearly mentioned in the *Bhagavad-gītā* that a true *sannyasin*, who has renounced the world, practices renunciation in action, not renunciation of action.

Puruṣārthas and the Other

The goals of human life (*puruṣārthas)* are meant to lead a contended life by the individuals in the society. The life becomes completely unsatisfied if these basic aims of human life are not fulfilled. They are *dharma, artha, kāma,* and *mokṣa.* The very meaning and purpose of human life, according to classical Indian philosophers, is well defined by these *puruṣārthas*. Since society is a dynamic organization wherein variety of human relations exist, there is an apparent need for proper social organization of these relations for the benefit of everyone. 'I' and 'other' have equal share and responsibility in maintaining proper social order. Thus *dharma* as a higher value acts as an overarching principle or regulative mechanism to extend *artha* and *kāma* in their proper proportion to the individuals. The highest value, *mokṣa*, is completely independent of *dharma*. What is higher cannot regulate the highest.

As pragmatic human beings all of us want to enjoy *artha*, and *kāma*. But our desire for material wealth and enjoyment of sensuous pleasures must have some limit. These limits are shown by *dharma*. A qualitatively good life encompasses all the four. But it is left to the individual (s) whether they can aspire for *mokṣa* or not. But certainly people do not want to forego *artha* and *kāma*. However, these two base values need a regulative principle like *dharma* to control the greed of the individuals. In the absence *dharma*, there is every possibility of such a society turning into Hobbesian state of nature wherein we find war of all against all. The existence of *dharma* as a regulative principle implies that the society is a conglomerate of many individuals. The other becomes part of such a society. Having admitted that human beings are combinations of material and spiritual elements, it is necessary to satisfy their material and spiritual needs. With respect to society, *dharma* provides the rules of conduct for settling the disputes and conflicts that arise in the course of social life of individuals. If the conflicts are kept in their minimum then the society can be well maintained. Thus *dharma* has an important role to play.

It is also true that human beings do not just live on righteousness and justice. They require both means of life (*artha*) and sensual enjoyment (*kāma*) for they are natural to any social life. Kautilya in his *Arthaśāstra* writes: "The sustenance of mankind is termed *artha*, the earth that contains mankind is *artha*..."[8] Etymologically, the word *'artha'* is derived from the Sanskrit root '*ri*' which means 'that which one goes after'. From this one can interpret *artha* as anything that is sought after. As ordinary social beings we aspire for wealth, position, profit, property, precious things and so on. Further, it is found in the *Mahābhārata* and in the *Pañchatantra* one's attitude towards *artha*. According to the former:

> What is regarded as *dharma* here depends entirely upon wealth (*artha*). One who robs another of wealth robs him of his *dharma* as well. Poverty is a state of sinfulness. All kinds of meritorious acts flow from the possession of great wealth, as from wealth spring all religious acts, all pleasures, and heaven itself. Wealth brings about accession to wealth, as elephants capture elephants. Religious acts, pleasure, joy, courage, worth, and learning; all these proceed from wealth. From wealth one's merit increases. He that has no wealth has neither this world nor the next.[9]

Even the traditional collection of tales of wisdom known as the *Pañchatantra* highlights following advantages of wealth. To quote from it: "The smell of wealth (*artha*) is quite enough to wakeup creature's sterner stuff. And wealth's enjoyment is even more. Wealth gives constant rigour, confidence, and power. Poverty is a curse worse than death. Virtue without wealth is of no consequence. The lack of money is the root cause of all evil."[10]

The above passages from the *Mahābhārata* and the *Pañchatantra* should not be misunderstood. *Artha* as one of the goals of human life refers to all necessarily means of life for comfortable living. What is emphasized here is the means to biological and social life of individuals. In other words, biological and social life are the prerequisites for spiritual life. It is *dharma* which monitors the misuse of *artha*. Therefore no *artha* is pursued in violation of *dharma*. Mere accumulation of wealth is not an end in itself. *Artha* is only a means to enjoyment (*kāma*). Human beings seek a sense of satisfaction, pleasure and enjoyment in their social life. In the absence of *kāma* life is bland and insipid. In the *Vātsāyanasūtra, kāma* is defined as follows:

> *Kāma* is the enjoyment of the appropriate objects of the five senses of hearing, feeling, seeing, tasting, and smelling, assisted by the mind, together with the soul. The ingredient in this is a peculiar contact between the organ of sense and its object, and the consciousness of the pleasure that results from the contact is called *kāma*.[11]

While discussing the relation among *dharma, artha,* and *kāma*, Manu writes:

> Some declare that the good of man consists in *dharma* and *artha;* others opine that it is found in *artha* and *kāma*; some say that

> *dharma* alone will give it; the rest assert that *artha* alone is the chief good of man here below. But the correct positon is that the good of man consists in the harmonious co-ordination of the three.[12]

It is natural for sensible human beings to strive for the satisfaction of their desires for food, drink, clothing, sex, and other sensual pleasures. The denial of sensual pleasures may lead to frustration and there is a chance an individual becoming a pervert. Instead, the sensuous pleasures have to be regulated. In a way the indulgence in sensual pleasures through regulated desires will make an individual active. In the absence of activity social life becomes dull and bored. The fourth and the most important human goal is *mokṣa*. Etymologically, the word '*mokṣa*' is derived from the Sanskrit root '*muc*' means 'to release' or 'to free'. After fulfilling the material desires of an individual sets himself or herself for the spiritual quest. According to the *Upaniṣads,* Ātman is the power behind the powers of the universe. If this were the case then the ultimate perfection of man is possible only through self-realization. Such realization sets man free from bondage. There is no death for Ātman, the power behind the universe. An individual has to transcend his or her biological and social existence to reach the spiritual heights. In fact, man has all the inbuilt potency within himself to realize the supreme Self. He has to translate this potency into actuality in order to realize his spiritual existence too.

Concluding Remarks

The other in Indian philosophical tradition has a positive effect on the growth of the individual as well as society. The classical Indian philosophers always directed their analysis of the other with a positive outlook. The negative consequences of the other cannot be ignored; but there are measures to control them in any welfare society through various methods of punishment as envisaged by the classical Indian ethical theories. Our own parents, teachers, kith and kin, friends and foes, and even God is the other. Can we dispense with them in our social life to enjoy the life as a solitary reaper? Imagine the kind of punishment meted to a hardened criminal when he is isolated from the rest and confined to a solitary cell in the jail. The kind of excommunication that he faces is worse than hell. One is deprived of one's social contacts with the other. Solitude is a curse. The knife that we use is meant for cutting fruits and vegetables, but it can also be used to stab others. Similarly, the other has positive and negative dimensions. As social beings we tap the positive qualities of the other, and the other is the most precious jewel in our social life.

Notes

1. *ChāndogyaUpaniṣad,* 6.2.1.
2. *Ibid.,* 6.4.5.6.
3. *Māṅḍūkya Upaniṣad,* 2.
4. R.N. Dandekar, "The Role of Man in Hinduism, " in *The Religion of the Hindus*, Kenneth Morgan (ed.), Delhi: Motilal Banarsidass, 1987, p. 117.
5. *Īśa Upaniṣad,* 1.6.7.16.
6. *The Mahābhārata, Śānti-parva,* 86.
7. *The Bhagavad-gītā,* 4.
8. John M Koller, *Oriental Philosophies*. New York: Charles Scribner's Sons, 1970, p. 36.
9. *Ibid.*
10. *Ibid.,* pp. 42-43.
11. *Ibid.*
12. *Ibid.*

11

The Integral Philosophy of Sri Aurobindo

Introduction

Arabinda Akryod Ghose (1872-1970), later known as Sri Aurobindo, is a one of the gifted philosophers of the Indian sub-continent. Unlike his other compeers Sri Aurobindo had a thorough western upbringing and education. However, Sri Aurobindo showed keen interest in the study of Indian culture in its entirety. In the process he assimilated and interpreted it with a view to provide a new orientation to Indian culture. He simply brushed aside the conception of westerners which dubs Indian culture as a form of occultism or superstition. After his active participation in the freedom struggle for about ten years he moved to Pondicherry, the then French territory, and devoted himself to the study of philosophy, integral yoga, meditation and spiritual experimentation for about forty long years and wrote copiously on these matters until his death in 1950.

During his early days in Pondicherry he was busy with his journal *The Arya* (1914-20) in which he published extensively on different subjects. His writings are the living testimony for his intellectual acumen. Later on these writings are brought together, partly revised, in the form of books. The notable among them are: *Essays on the Gītā, Synthesis of Yoga, The Human Cycle, The Ideal of Human Unity,* and his *magnum opusThe Life Divine*. Apart from these, there are also two volumes of *Collected Poems*, and his great epic *Savitri*, which is written in about twenty seven thousand lines. One who reads it would attain the mystic sublimity. By and large, his writings focus on the evolution of the world, and of man, through different stages. His integral yoga presupposes the divine destiny of man. As observed by Dasgupta: "A harmonious and integral culture of his physical, vital and mental potentialities alone enables man to rise to a supramental realization of Truth, transforming and divinizing his total being. Man can thus become a superman, thinking, feeling and acting in unison, with the Divine."[1]

In this essay an attempt is made to provide a comprehensive account of Sri Aurobindo's philosophy.

Epistemology

The metaphysical presuppositions of any philosopher are justified through his epistemological framework. Sri Aurobindo is not an exception to this rule. He considers experience in its widest sense in order to accommodate knowledge obtained through different sources of experience.[2] Hardcore epistemologists confine their experience to mere sense experience. For them it is something ultimate and no other form of experience is acceptable to them. Thus all knowledge is generated out of sense-object contact. But, for Sri Aurobindo, this ordinary sense-experience is only a middle part of our existence. It is sandwiched between subconscious and super-conscious spheres. In our sleeping state we retire into the former state of experience. Sometimes it also forms as the background in our waking state in which the automatic vital functions take place for the sustenance of the waking life. Also, we receive occasional flashes (moments of intuition) from the super-conscious sphere. These moments of intuition make us feel that we are one with the sublime (the Self). This is the typical character of a spiritual experience. To quote Sri Aurobindo here: "An integral knowledge demands an exploration, an unveiling of all the possible domains of consciousness and experience."[3] Sri Aurobindo attempts to explore, interpret and integrate all such data.

Sri Aurobindo reconstructs the ancient Vedāntic conception of reality in its new light to suit the later mentality. Both in the *Upaniṣads* and the *Gītā* the five organs of sense, lower mind (*manas*), and higher mind (*buddhi*) are described as the sources of human knowledge. However, the Self, which is self-luminous, is place above these three. The later Indian systems developed these ideas differently. However, Sri Aurobindo hardly gives any importance to later developments. According to him, the senses are only the specializations of the outward mind. It is mind, out of ignorance, divides the Self from the external world. The truth is that the Self and the external world are one and the same. The day-to-day practical affairs pressurise the mind to establish this sundered relation through the senses which are its own outward forms. Strictly speaking, for Sri Aurobindo, the mind is the real sense underlying all other senses. Mind has the capacity to work independently of the senses. The mind is capable of reaching the objects of the external world without the aid of senses. This is seen "in experiments of hypnosis and cognate psychological phenomena."[4] In these cases the waking mind is put to sleep and the genuine or subliminal mind operates. Thus the true character of mind is revealed. In other words, the powers of mind are far superior to those of senses.

Sri Aurobindo is not primarily interested to extend the powers of mind to know the nature of phenomenal world. He is more interested in those truths which are beyond sense perception, but can be captured by the perceptions of reason.[5] An inquiry into the operations of reason reveals that reason has two activities to perform. They are: mixed and pure. In its mixed activity the reason gathers data of the external world from sense-experience in order to interpret and interrelate them to arrive at different kinds of inferences. This is typically the way in which the reason operates in the scientific realm. But reason in its pure form tries to transcend these ordinary perceptual experiences and "strives to arrive at general or unalterable concepts which attach themselves not to the appearances of things, but to that which stands behind their appearances."[6] By going beyond the ordinary level of sense-experiences man uses his superior gift of reason which distinguishes man from rest of the living creatures. Thus the "complete use of pure reason brings us finally from physical to metaphysical knowledge."[7] But these concepts of pure reason may not satisfy the demands of our integral being, for all ideas are mere promises of possible immediate experiences. These promises have to be fulfilled by proper verification mechanism. There must be some immediate non-sensuous experience which verifies all the ideas of pure reason. Is such experience possible? Sri Arubindo's reply to this question is positive. Direct or non-sensuous experience of the reality which exists beyond ordinary sense-experience reveals us that this reality is within every one of us in an obscure way. It can be developed through proper culture. Intuitively we know about our own existence. One does not require the mediation of senses or mind to know that one exists. Here we acquire knowledge of our own existence by means of identity or by knowing just by being. In this context Sri Aurobindo reminds us that: "Ancient Vedānta seized this message of the intuition and formulated it in the three great declarations of the Upaniṣads, 'I am He', 'Thou art That', O Swetaketu', 'All this is the Brahman; this self is the Brahman'."[8]

Intuition is not a process, and it cannot be articulated. It is only reason which organises, analyses and interprets the message of intuition. Reason also interprets the phenomena and our surface being in relation to intuitive, noumenal truths to construct systems of metaphysics as per the demands of our rational nature. But when metaphysics ignores its intuitive base it is lost "in the clouds because it deals with words as if they were imperative facts instead of symbols."[9] Thus rival schools or doctrines of metaphysics surface. Of course, Sri Aurobindo does not deny the fact that intuitions too vary with each other in terms of their content, depth and fullness. But each one of them possesses a self-corrective mechanism within itself. Just as one sense-experience is corrected by another better sense-experience, so also "the less luminous gives place to the more luminous, the narrower, faultier or less essential to the more comprehensive, more perfect, more essential."[10] Reason can never replace intuition. It can only interpret the content of an intuition to enlighten the surface mind.

Sri Aurobindo puts forward a fourfold order of knowledge. There is a gradual transformation of intuition which results in separative knowledge. First, there is knowledge by identity which results from our immediate awareness of our self-luminous self. One does not find any sense of separation in this form of knowledge for one is complete engrossed in emotion or thought. Then there is knowledge by intimate direct contact when we partly disengage ourselves from the states and observe them while they are continuing. The third type is knowledge by separative direct contact in which the observer separates himself from the stream of metal states and assume the role of a witness. Finally, we observe external objects external objects through senses. Here the knower and the known are completely separated from each other. Here we need the mediation of senses to obtain the knowledge of the objects of the external world. If we can descend from the highest level of knowledge to the lowest level, then it is also possible to ascend from the lower level to the higher. We can do this when we philosophically convinced by the reason that man and world, the knower and the known are only the partial expressions of the same reality. By overcoming these polarities we arrive at the unity of total being with the total reality. Such knowledge alone is integral, according to Sri Aurobidno. Integral knowledge leads to integral transformation of the human personality. In order to understand this there is a need to understand his metaphysics which takes into account the theory of evolution.

Metaphysics

Sri Aurobdnso's metaphysics views God, nature and man, and man's social duties as a synthetic whole. His *Essays on the Gĩtā*, and *The Life Divine* discuss these aspects. For Sri Aurobindo, philosophy is to discover that being by knowing which everything else is known.[11] This monistic ideal is also pursued by science by reaching the most general laws and principles which would explain the diversity and multiplicity of phenomena. Thus science has come to realise the existence of matter, force and energy underlying the both. The achievements of science, holds Sri Aurobindo, are great within its self-limited area of inquiry. But scientific truth alone cannot be treated as a paradigm of all knowledge. The inadequacies of materialism exposed when science tries to explain the origin of the universe in terms of some unconscious factors. It fails to acknowledge man's deeper spiritual experiences and higher destiny for want of evidence in terms of scientific measurements. Sri Aurobindo cautions us that in the name of mysticism and spirituality obscure, crude and spurious doctrines have been advanced. Mysticism and spiritual experience cannot be brought down to the level of ordinary formal logic; they have transcendental logic of their own.

The supreme reality of Sri Aurobindo is *Sat-Cit-Ǎnanda*. But this Absolute is not an isolated entity in the sense that we must rationally understand and explain its relation to the ordinary world of experiences (the finite world). The advaitic conception of the Absolute, which is indeterminate, is beset with some contradictions, according to Sri Aurobindo. How does a pure unity devoid of all attributes give rise to the world of appearances or multiplicity? The advaitins put forward the argument that the absolute reality being pure is the only reality. The world of empirical existence is only an illusion. This explanation of advaitins is not satisfactory for it ignores the world of empirical existence instead of explaining it. Even an illusion must have some reality for its ground and this ground must have some characteristics. Although the Absolute is indeterminate and transcendent, holds Sri Aurobindo, it is capable of gradual creative self-expression and self-determination. To put it in the words of Sri Aurobindo: "It is perfectly understandable that the absolute is and must be indeterminable in the sense that it cannot be limited by any determination, or any sum of possible determinations, but not in the sense that it is incapable of self-determination."[12] The Absolute cannot be described in terms of any quality or property or power for they cannot fully explain its nature. Advaitins described the Absolute negatively. But, argues Sri Aurobindo, such negation in another way limits the absolute by denying it even the freedom of self-expression and self-determination.[13] The problem is that *Upaniṣads* describe Brahman negatively, yet they declare it to be positive by holding the view that "All this is Brahman". This contradictory nature of the Absolute is inconceivable to reason. Are not advaitins, questions Sri Aurobindo, driven by the logic of contradictions?

Sri Aurobindo argues that both negative and positive attributes cannot be ascribed to the Absolute. The Absolute is a positive entity and has its own transcendental logic. There is "a greater reason in all the operations of the Infinite, but it is not a mental or intellectual, it is spiritual or supramental reason: there is logic in it because there are relations and connections in fallibly seen and executed; what is the magic to our finite reason is the logic of the Infinite."[14] The Infinite is ineffable for it is a harmonious unity of indeterminate, immutable, infinite aspects and is immanent, determinate, and dynamic in its finite aspects. The triune nature of the Absolute is constituted by pure existence (*sat*), pure consciousness (*cit*) and pure bliss (*ānanda*). The individual soul, its mind, life and body evolve out of the Absolute by a process of self-manifestation through multiple self-limitation and self-differentiation. This process of self-limitation is what is called '*māyā*' by the early Vedānta. One of the most interesting features of Sri Aurobindo's philosophy is his analysis of the notion of evolution which explicates this process of the self-manifestation of the absolute.

Evolution

Even before the scientists have formulated any theory of evolution, the concept of evolution found its place in the Indian tradition. In the *Taittirīya Upaniṣad* it is mentions as follows:

> In the beginning all this Universe was Non-existent and unmanifest from which this manifest was born. Itself created itself; none other created it. Therefore, they say of it the well and beautifully made.[15]

Similarly, Sāṅkhya, one of the orthodox systems of Indian tradition propounded a theory of evolution. According to this system, Prakṛti and Puruṣa are two realities. The proximity of the former to the latter disturbed the equilibrium of *guṇas, sattva, rajas* and *tamas* of Prakṛti. This resulted in the evolution of the various phenomena. But Sri Aurobindo puts forward a completely different thesis concerning evolution in order to show what unique insights could be provided by philosophers as metaphysicians. He discussed his views on evolution very systematically in his *The Life Divine*. In fact, Sri Aurobindo's integral philosophy rests on his spiritual theory of evolution. He started his discussion on evolution with an important note that "there seems to be no reason why Life should not evolve out of material elements or Mind out of living forms, unless we accept the Vedāntic solution that life is already involved in matter and mind in life...."[16] Most of the modern evolutionists ignored this point. The principle of evolution towards Spirit, Light and Knowledge loses all its significance unless it is assumed that the Spirit itself has involved in matter, darkness and ignorance. This amounts to saying that evolution necessarily involves involution, the ascent by descent. This is the unique feature of Sri Aurobindo's theory of evolution.

In order to make his point clear, first of all, Sri Aurobindo attacked both materialist and idealist theories of evolution for their apparent inconsistencies. There is self-contradiction in materialism, for it cannot explain how an unconscious principle evolves into life and consciousness from it. Both Darwin and Spencer spoke of adaptation between an individual and his environment, but human individual cannot accept his environment as fixed and determined forever. Similarly, idealist theories held the view that reason is the highest stage of evolution. If it were so, then there is no evolution beyond reason. Contrary to these two approaches, Sri Aurobindo's theory of evolution is a balanced approach based on spiritual and humanistic principles. For his, the Spirit, which is supreme Reality, is the source of creation and evolution, and also the end of realization. The Spirit evolves out of matter since it is already implicit in it. Thus Sri Aurobindo opposed extremism in both materialist and idealist theories.

The supreme Reality, according to Sri Aurobindo, is *Sat-Cit-Ǎnanda.* It is both stable and dynamic. In other words, it is an integration of Being and becoming. The reality of the world is due to the manifestation of the Divine Unity in the world. The higher 'involves' itself in the lower and inconsistent so as to evolve out of it in a double line process. Sri Aurobindo's theory of evolution centres around his concept of 'Conscious-Force'. According to him, creation is due to this force which is active. He calls it Life-Force or Divine *Śakti*. It is the power behind all creation. The supreme Reality is one without the second. Both spirit and matter are real as there is Brahman in them.[17] Brahman is both transcendent and immanent. Brahman is being absolute cannot be described. According to Sri Aurobidno, "The ascent to the divine Life is the human journey, the work of works, the acceptable sacrifice."[18] The descent or involution is self-concealing, while the ascent or the evolution is self-unveiling of the Reality. However, we must note that there are successive levels of descending journey of the Reality. There are several stages through which Reality gradually veils itself. Similarly, there is a progressive development in the ascending journey. The revelation or the unveiling of the Reality has to cross many steps leading to total realization. So far we have noticed the three important stages in the process of evolution. They are the stages of matter, of life and of mind. At present we are living in the mental plane. Sri Aurobindo states that we have these three particular stages of evolution only due to the downward march of involution. The downward march followed the very same stages from mind to life, and from life to matter. This is the reason why Sri Aurobindo considers the problem of creation as important as the problem of evolution.

The second unique feature of Sri Aurobindo's theory of evolution is that it solves the puzzle that constantly plagued most of the evolutionists. Scientists failed in their attempt to explain the growth of life in inert matter. Reality, as a Conscious-Force, involves itself in the material ignorance by the process of self-concealing, then matter is nothing but Spirit in a different form. Even this so called inert matter is potentially endowed with that Conscious-Force which is inherent in the supreme Reality. This explanation of Sri Aurobindo helps in understanding the growth of life in matter. As mentioned above, both in descent as well as in ascent, there are several steps. The following is the order mentioned by Sri Aurobindo.

The descent starts from Truth or Spirit and reaches matter through Conscious-Force, bliss, supermind, mind, psyche, and life. Sri Aurobindo talks of certain minor links that connect mind and supermind. They are higher mind, illumined mind, intuitive mind and overmind. This is the order in which the progressive manifestation of the Reality takes place in the Universe. To quote Sri Aurobindo:

> For each successive level of descent to the Divine is to man a stage in an ascent; each veil that hides the unknown God becomes for the God-lover and God –seeker an instrument for His unveiling.[19]

Sri Aurobndo's theory of evolution is neither mechanistic nor purposive. He clearly states why the Reality plunges into darkness or ignorance. *Sat-Cit-Ănanda* is everything and has everything already in Him. There is nothing left for supreme Reality to be accomplished. As Sri Aurobidno puts it, "All is a game or '*Lĩlā*'; but a game too carries within itself an object to be accomplished and without the fulfilment of that object would have no completeness of significance."[20] Therefore, it is a predestined denouncement. The process of evolution, according to Sri Aurobindo, is a triple "process of heightening, widening and integration."[21] This is the most original contribution of Sri Aurobindo to evolution. It is a heightening process as it raises upwards to higher and higher levels. Matter raises to life, and life to mind and so on. Along with the process of heightening, the process of evolution widens also. As soon as a new principle emerges within the old ones it is given accommodation for its subsistence. For instance, when the principle of life emerges, matter sufficiently widens itself to accommodate life in it. The third process in evolution is integration. With the process of heightening, and widening, the lower principles are not neglected instead the higher ones get integrated with the lower ones. In this context to quote Sri Aurobindo:

> Our mental, physical, vital existence need not be destroyed by our self-exceeding, nor or they lessened and impaired by being spiritualised; they can and do become much richer, greater, more powerful and more perfect.[22]

Thus evolution is never an isolated rising into higher principle, but it is also a total transformation of all the lower principles. So it is not a partial raising of the world process, but a radical uplift towards higher forms of existence. For an evolution to bė perfect it must be complete in itself. In other words, it must be thorough and radical transformation of all the principles of the world. This is another salient feature that we come across in Sri Aurobindo's theory of evolution. The outcome of this triple process of evolution is cosmic salvation. However, the role of individual soul cannot be ignored in this evolutionary development. According to Sri Aurobindo: "In the previous stages of revolution Nature's first care and effort had to be directed towards a change in the physical organisation."[23] Its is due to this reason that the world process "stated without consciousness and without individuality in an undifferentiated form."[24] But it is through the individual consciousness and transmutation that the evolution can be effected.

The movement of evolution is the progressive self-manifestation of the Spirit in the material universe. The fact is that man is often ignorant of his divinity and is unable to foresee the future possibilities. Spiritual evolution for Sri Aurobindo means the transformation of the life of ignorance into the Divine life of Truth-Consciousness. In the process of evolution, the spiritual man emerges out of the man of mental being. If man is not to remain as a mere phenomenal being he has to understand the four truths about himself. First of all, man must know his potentialities and must utilise them. Secondly, he must dive deep below his physical and mental surface into his inner psychic powers. Thirdly, he must know the power that controls the world, namely, the Spirit or the Creator. Lastly, he must know how to live himself above the present imperfections and limitations. This shows that by slowly unfolding himself, man can discover his divinity in and through the phenomenal world. Thus Sri Aurobindo is both a spiritualist and humanist.

Coming to the process of evolution, Sri Aurobindo holds that it is the logical necessity that if something has involved it must naturally evolve back to its origin. Evolution of life into matter is possible only when the life is already present there in the matter. Evolution of life to mind is possible only when the mind is already contained in the life, and the evolution of mind to supermind is possible only when the latter is inherent in the former. The triple transformation which Sri Aurobindo talks of is ultimately necessary to conclude the evolutionary process. This triple transformation includes the psychic change, the spiritual change, and the crowning moment, namely, the ascent into supermind. The first two changes are preparatory stages for the third. Once we achieve this stage, the suptramental light will radiate the whole of our nature and being.

Thus against materialist and idealist theories of evolution, Sri Aurobindo advanced a spiritual one, the roots of which can be traced back to the grand *Upaniṣadic* tradition. His theory of evolution is cyclical, but not continuous. In the case of latter, evolution is a continuous process from lower to higher forms. Thus it is teleological. But Sri Aurobindo did not attribute any teleological necessity to his theory of evolution. However, he accommodates teleology in a different form. Once the involution takes place, the evolution necessarily becomes purposive as it has to reach its original state. This is unavoidable. At the same time Sri Aurobindo's theory of evolution can be treated as an emergent type for he admits that supramental consciousness is matter of emergence, a sudden and uncertain occurrence. Not only that, Sri Aurobindo's fundamental presupposition is that anything that emerges must be located in the cause. Such a view goes close to the *satkārya-vāda*, according to which the effect must pre-exist in the cause.

Scientific theories of evolution rely on the observable data which are restricted to appearances alone. The Reality, which is spiritual cannot be apprehended by scientific investigation. This is where science fails miserably. Objectivity alone cannot explain everything. With our finite logic we cannot apprehend the infinite. All our attempts result in a failure when we venture to apply finite logic to the infinite. The infinite has its own logic. The infinite can be experienced and can be felt. But it cannot be investigated into.

Social Philosophy

It is totally unfair on the part of those who imagine that the spiritual philosophers in general, who are often branded as hardcore metaphysicians or mystics, show no concern for the immediate existential crises faced by human individuals in their day-to-day life, for they are always interested in extramandane human concerns like attaining self-perfection or liberation or salvation from the shackles of the phenomenal world. Such an attitude towards spiritual philosophers is largely the result of the misconceived notion of the expression 'spiritual'. Often people fail to distinguish between religion and spirituality. The former is only a doctrinaire and denominational interested in spreading a belief system of its own, and the latter is a kind of disposition or attitude, a disciplined way of life through which one can attain spiritual awakening. Such a state is often contrasted with the materialist form of life. A spiritualist need not be an anti-materialist, but a contended materialist. He is one who strikes a proper balance between the spiritual and material pursuits and urges. For instance, blind adherence to materialism leads to fetishism[25] at the cost of human values, and the rigid pursuit of spiritualism may end up in abstract and empty transcendentalism.[26] It is in the social philosophy of Sri Aurobidno we come across a harmonious blend of these two dichotomous ways. The lack of contentment in one's life leads to greed and proliferation of egoistic desires that are root cause of social disharmony. In fact, the expression 'spirituality' in the classical Indian tradition stands for fearlessness, purity, steadfastness in knowledge and concentration, charity, self-restraint, worship, austerity, uprightness, non-violence, truth, absence of anger, renunciation, serenity, absence of calumny, compassion, non-covetousness, gentleness, modesty, absence of fickleness, energy, forgiveness, fortitude, absence of hatred and absence of pride.[27] Unless one is circumspect enough to distinguish between religion[28] and spirituality, there is a great danger of assimilating one with the other. It has become, more or less, a fashion to claim to be rational and scientific. Of course, no one denies the importance of rationality and scientific objectivity, but our effort to reduce everything to reason and scientific outlook becomes an unwarranted obsession for rationality and scientific objectivity. Consequently, spirituality is often treated as something irrational, and antithetical to science. Most of the modern writers under the influence of modern science started using the expression 'spiritual' in its pejorative and degenerative senses. As aptly held by Immanuel Kant in his *Critique of Pure Reason,* the things-in-themselves belong to the noumenal realm and are not subjected to discursive rational analysis. Pure reason fails to analyze their nature, for they are neither concepts nor percepts of our ordinary empirical experience. The noumenal realm consists of God, freedom, and morality for Kant. They are guided by our practical reason. To realize them one has to lead religious, free, and moral life. Similarly, spirituality is also a thing-in-itself to be realized by leading a spiritual way of life. One can approach spirituality by practicing the spiritual way of life rather than engaging in analyzing discursively what spirituality is. Similar view is expressed by Wittgenstein in his *Tractatus* when he held that there are no values in the world, for the world consists of only facts of existence. If at all there are values they exist outside the world. In other words, values are not subjected to any logical analysis for they are cultivated. Therefore, our judgments about values are neither true nor false. Like other human values, spirituality as a human value is cultivated. As a higher value spirituality subsumes all other values under it.

Sri Aurobindo's social philosophy is an outcome of his metaphysics. In his metaphysics Sri Aurobindo accords the highest status to the One (*Sat-Cit- Ǎnanda*), which undergoes the process of involution before it evolves into a multiplicity of individual centres representing the various stages of human development. Although Sri Aurobindo emphasizes the role of individual in society he rejects extreme form of individualism which regards individual(s) as the highest or prior to reality, and society as an artificial or convenient aggression of individuals. Sri Aurobindo firmly believes that there is no historical evidence to show that man existed without any society. At the same time he rejects the extreme form of collectivism which regards society as a primary and fundamental reality, and individuals as only its parts or cells. According to him, both man and society have equal status in the scheme of evolution for they are the expressions of the supreme Reality (*Sat-Cit-Ănanda*). Entire universe, humanity, society, and individuals are all the manifestations of the supreme Reality. An individual loses his/her identity in isolation from the society in which he/she is born, for the individual needs the support of the society for the expansion of his/her physical, vital and mental being. As a matter of fact, state, society or any other social or political organization, according to Sri Aurobindo, are only instruments through which an individual realizes the ultimate Reality. Also, it is only through the individual development the progress of any society or humankind in general is visualized.[29] The ultimate objective of all social, political, and human organizations is to help each other to evolve to the level of supramental consciousness. Such an experience turns each individual into a universal spiritual individual. With this end in view Sri Aurobindo proceeds to analyze the basic human nature.

Like any other contemporary Indian social philosopher, Sri Aurobindo tries to analyze the basic human nature in order to assess the place, status, and role of human individual in society. According to him, human individual's being has both inner and outer dimensions. The inner being of every individual represents his/her spiritual component and the outer materialistic. Thus both the inner and outer beings are integrated into one single being. The existential crises encountered by human individuals in the contemporary society are due to the fact that the inner being of man is completely ignored or neglected or relegated to the background. The undue importance given to the outer being of man resulted in the lopsided development of human nature as such. The egoistic desires and the ambitious pursuits to fulfil those desires of human beings, which are basically self-centered, represent the core of man's outer being. Consequently, men fail to distinguish between what is desired and what is desirable.[30] The domination of the former over the latter results in social disharmony. To maintain perfect social harmony, men must realize the importance of what is desirable for the larger interests of the society in which every individual stands to benefit or gain. Hence, asserts Sri Aurobindo, the need of the hour is to control and transform one's inner nature (being) in order to prepare oneself for the new society, which is an embodiment of altruism. He observes that: "The erringr ace of human beings dream always of perfecting their environment by the machinery of government and society; but it is only by the perfection of the soul within that the outer environment can be perfected."[31]

Sri Aurobindo's social philosophy is an offshoot of his spiritual humanism or integral philosophy, which is also characterized as socio-spiritualism that provides a synthetic view of life as such. While giving a detailed account of the assent of consciousness from its base level to the supramental level, he questioned the very foundations of the scientific theories of evolution to propose an alternative theory that not only explains the process of human evolution in terms of the gradations of mind, [32] the involution of the pure self or consciousness (*Sat-Cit-Ănanda*). According to him, the process of evolution appears to be meaningless unless we take into account the process of involution. In a way, evolution necessarily involves involution. This background would help us in understanding Sri Aurobindo's views on individual, society, and state.

Sri Aurobindo's spiritualism is not narrow in the sense that it is neither creedal nor sectarian. His spiritualism not only takes into account the life of the senses, but also rejects the escapist tendencies. It rather affirms life and is equally sensitive to beauty and joy. The spiritualism of Sri Aurobindo is not different from his socio-political activities and is not bereft of the sense of history. His spiritualism is also conscious of our inescapable involvement in socio-political, economic and cultural life of the society in which we live. It only helps us transcending the triviality of this day-to-day life pattern in order to make our life more meaningful, authentic, purposeful and perfect. The salient feature of such a kind of spiritualism is that it does not overlook natural and material base of life and society. All these aspects are integrated into one single unit to arrive at an ideal human society.

The most interesting thing to be noticed in Sri Aurobindo's spiritual and integral philosophy is his concern for man and the natural and social reality in which man lives. Sri Aurobindo felt for man, worked for man, and aimed at better and brighter future of man. The real motto behind his spiritual philosophy is to inspire man to seek self-realization with a view to achieve self-perfection which, directly or indirectly, has its own role to play in human society. Plato in his

Republic held that a just society consists of just individuals. And a just individual is one who is able conquer his irrational part of the soul, which is dominated by spirit and appetite, with the rational part of his soul that is dominated by reason. If it happens otherwise, then a human being is reduced to the level of a beast. Analogically, in Sri Aurobindo's integral philosophy it is the individual who has to strive for perfection which automatically results in social perfection, for the perfect society consists of perfect individuals.

Sri Aurobindo firmly believes that the ascent of consciousness from lower to higher, and from higher to the highest level explains the fundamental principle of human evolution in which the pure spirit or consciousness (*Sat-Cit-Ǎnanda*), which is One, diversifies itself into multiplicity of individual centres. The very purpose of such diversification is to regain its original status. The entire process ultimately culminates in the evolution of a spiritual individual.[33]Sri Aurobindo envisages that both man and society are interdependent and complimentary to each other, but not mutually exclusive. The metaphysical dimension provided by Sri Aurobindo to explain the relation between individual and society amounts to fusion of sociality with spirituality. Further he views that every individual is born into a society and necessarily needs the support of society in which he/she is born to develop his/her personality in terms of physical, vital and mental being. The metaphysical approach of Sri Aurobindo towards individual and society is not totally bereft of logic. He recognizes the concept of 'unity' in his social philosophy. According to him, the question of unity arises provided that there is something called 'diversity'. Although there is an apparent polarity between these two concepts, they are not antithetical to each other rather they derive their significance from each other. Sri Aurobindo foresees that the ideal of all the legitimate human organizations is to look for unity in rich diversity. This is the essence of his integral philosophy. But, the question arises: How is unity possible? Does the rich diversity allow any unity among the individuals? Sri Aurobindo's answer to this question is positive. He feels that it is only through spiritual means the humanity as a whole can be united.

Like his forerunners in the Indian philosophical tradition, Sri Aurobindo is of the opinion that as long as an individual lives in ignorance of his own self, which is the supreme Principle, he is always controlled by his physical, vital, mental, and intellectual urges and impulses. These urges and impulses exhibit themselves in the form of desires that make an individual selfish and egocentric. This is the starting point of all social problems and evils. In order to contain these social evils, individuals living in a society or state must frame rules and laws. It becomes indispensable for a society or a state, which is based on materialistic outlook, to legislate certain laws in order to maintain itself. Thus governmental machinery, as an external force, is used to maintain social cohesion. The strong regimentation of rules and the laws imposed by the governmental machinery necessarily curbs the free growth of the individual. Of course, Sri Aurobindo concedes this point. However, a genuine unity or harmony among the individuals is possible only through spiritual means. As a matter of fact, the law of unity or harmony is inherent in the very law of the spirit. Thus, maintains Sri Aurobindo, the social cohesion achieved by external means is only temporary and evanescent, while the unity or harmony achieved by means of spiritual power is enduring.

What is expected of an individual is to feel oneself with the spirit or the supreme Principle, which is the underlying principle of all. By identifying oneself with the Spirit, one can get rid of one's ego and its selfish desires. Consequently, one can see the self in all selves, and vice-versa. The Spirit as a highest form of consciousness is chiefly responsible in bringing about harmony in feeling, thought, and action. It does not require any aid of intellect or calculation. It is a spontaneous activity by itself. Sri Aurobindo aptly envisages that the primary objective or goal of all social, political, and other human organizations is to help each other to evolve the supramental consciousness that leads to the immediate realization of the Divine.[34] Such as act ultimately turns every individual into a universal spiritual individual.

Of course, it is only to bring about social harmony, to promote altruism, and to curb egoistic impulses of ignorant individuals, a society or a state imposes certain rules, regulations, and the laws of morality on the individuals. But when the individual attains spiritual realization, he needs no guidelines from the society or the state in which he/she is a member, for all these externally imposed on him her become completely redundant. For an enlightened individual there exists no ego. Therefore, he is a free being. Being free from egoistic impulses and desires, he acts in harmony with the best interests of all for the furtherance of human race as such. The basic and the universal moral laws are the best expression of the spiritual truths of love and harmony. An enlightened or a spiritual individual never follows them as something externally imposed on him. They become part and parcel of his intrinsic nature. The sense of goodness spontaneously comes out of his integral knowledge. From the spiritual point of view he realizes that "good is all that helps the individual and the world towards their divine fullness, and evil is all that retards or breaks up that increasing perfection."[35]

What is interesting to note here is that Sri Aurobindo is also aware of the fact that what he propounds appears to be utopian and unrealistic. In order to defend his position he takes up these issues in historical, realistic, and evolutionary perspective in his highly illuminating works *The Human Cycle* and *The Ideal of Human Unity*. In the former work he elaborately discusses the way in which human culture and civilization are moulded and influenced by individualism, subjectivism, objectivism, aesthetics, ethics, infra-rational mind and reason. Each of these has its own shortcomings, yet each one of them has its own lessons to teach. In the latter, he narrates the transition of the different forms of state from monarchy to democracy and democracy to socialism. But all these stages have their own shortcomings for the state by its very nature is mechanical and soulless. In other words, the state does not give any importance to axiological and spiritual nature of man. Sometimes it unduly suppresses the creative mind of the individuals. Theoretically speaking it is the subordination of the individual for the collective good of everyone. But in practice "it is his (individual's) subordination to a collective egoism, political, military, economic, which seeks to satisfy certain collective aims and ambitions shaped and imposed on the great mass of the individuals by a smaller or a larger number of ruling persons who are supposed in some way to represent the community. There is no guarantee that the ruling class or ruling body represents the best mind of nation or its noblest aim or its highest instincts."[36]

Sri Aurobindo discusses at length and explicates the issues concerning human solidarity and unity in the light of the different actual and possible political organizations such as nations, states, empires, federations, world-empire. By and large, all these political organizations failed to deliver the goods to fulfil the dream of achieving liberty, equality, and fraternity. They are only the limited expressions of spiritual aspirations of humanity, and cannot be realized unless human organizations are based on spiritual ideals. Therefore, there is every need to build up a true religion of humanity that fosters the furtherance of human race. The divine presence in the form of supra-mental consciousness in very human being, irrespective of caste, creed, religion, region, language, race, and so on, alone can transform the society into a divine society. Just as Plato's just society consists of just individuals, Sri Aurobindo's divine society consists of divine individuals, who are the embodiment of spirituality. Only in such divine society the individuals can have deepest and spontaneous feeling of fraternity, which ensures liberty and equality for all. In this context Sri Aurobindo writes: "In all the higher powers of his life man may be said to be seeking, blindly enough, for God, the Eternal, the Self or Truth, Good and Beauty."[37] This many sided seeking of man definitely demands the radical evolution of man beyond reason to a supramental immediate consciousness of God capable of harmonizing the clashes of "multiplied excessive needs and desires and consequent conflicts among individuals and nations with vital and intellectual civilization has created."[38]

Sri Aurobindo digs at creedal religion for its indulgence in saving the individual from the burden of life without undertaking the venture of transforming life in the world. Moreover, religion as a human phenomenon got mixed up with lower impulses and is being abused for granting sanctions to vested interests, conventions, and institutions which often lack spiritual sanctity. According to Sri Aurobindo: "This false socialization of religion has always been the chief cause of its failure to regenerate mankind."[39] The religion that he aims at is a supramental or supra-rational spiritual religion that provides a complete integral education for man. Such an education includes the physical, the vital, the mental, the intellectual, the aesthetic, and many other important facts of human life. The ultimate goal of supramental spiritual religion is to reveal the presence of the divine in every aspect of human life, nature and in all other spheres of life. In every human faculty there is divine element that is responsible for a perfect growth of human personality.

Concluding Remarks

To conclude: *prima facie,* the spiritual humanism advocated by Sri Aurobindo appears to be utopian in its character. But it is not really so. The dictum "where there is will there is way" holds good in this context. Of course, one needs to make a distinction between what is practical and what is impractical. The latter is something that is beyond human ability or capability to perform or act under given circumstances. At the same time one needs to be more cautious about the distinction between what is practical, and what is deliberately made impractical by sheer human indifference. In a way it is non-utilization or improper utilization of inner human talents that is otherwise practical made totally impractical. For instance, all of us are concerned with global warming and climate change, but we do not have the commitment to put an end to this dangerous phenomenon. We are not prepared to change our lifestyle. Our lifestyle is Faustian lifestyle where we do not care for the future of our own race. The existential crises faced by the individuals in modern societies are the result of this human indifference. The importance given to modern science or scientific rationality at the cost of moral or spiritual life of individuals is bound to destroy the furtherance of human race on the globe. In his spiritual humanism, Sri Aurobindo opposed all forms of extremism. Like the Buddha and Aristotle, Sri Aurobindo treads the middle path or the principle of golden mean. According to him, both materialism and spiritualism are complementary to each other. A perfect blend of these two would certainly enhance the quality of human life. A genuine philosophical pursuit is one that aims at discovering the spiritual reality by means of which human existence can learn its own law of development and aim at perfection. However, Sri Aurobindo reiterates that perfection and completeness cannot be achieved from mere passive or negative attitude towards world and life. A true realization of the synthesis of the outer and the inner, the matter and the spirit would provide vivid picture of the world and life. In the integral philosophy of Sri Aurobindo the social takes the clue from the spiritual. They are not antithetical to each other. In fact they constitute the concrete man. The spiritual progress in man contributes to social progress. Similarly, the social progress shows the spiritual heights achieved by man. The vertical progress of man is reflected in the horizontal progress of society. This is true of all societies and nations. Social equality and better economic conditions cannot be restricted to a section of people. Unless they are guaranteed to entire humanity, the real social freedom is not achieved. In fact, the much discussed and debated doctrine of human rights is visualized by Sri Aurobindo long before its declaration by United Nations in 1948. He is of the opinion that individual freedom should not be restricted to mere social and political privileges, but must be extended to moral and spiritual life of the individuals. Individual freedom, according to Sri Aurobindo, does not consist in the satisfaction of one's ego or senses or in anarchical display of one's self-will. The real freedom consists in the domain of morality. The more we become moral, the more we become free. A perfect social order is the result of moral and spiritual freedom. What is enforced by any external agency or government machinery does not bring about true social order. A genuine social order is possible through the transformation of total human nature by being moral and spiritual, active and co-operative. He writes in *The Human Cycle:*"The true law of our development and the entire object of our social existence an only become clear to us when we have discovered not only, like modern science, what man has been in the past physical and vital evolution, but his future mental and spiritual destiny and his place in the cycles of Nature."[40] The integral philosophy of Sri Aurobindo is a perfect combination of pragmatic and spiritual aspirations of humankind. To put it in the language of modern human rights doctrine, the divine society envisaged by Sri Aurobindo is one such society that guarantees and upholds human dignity by treating human rights as universal obligations or responsibilities or commitments. His spiritual philosophy is truly a social philosophy of action.

Notes

1. Dhirendra Mohan Datta, *The Chief Currents of Contemporary Philosophy,* Culcatta: Calcutta University Press, 1970, 3rd edn., p. 152.
2. Sri Aurobindo, *The Life Divine,* Pondicherry: Sri Aurobindo Ashram, BK.1, Ch.III, p. 58f.
3. *Ibid.,* p. 581.
4. *Ibid.,* p. 61.

5. *Ibid.,* p. 62.
6. *Ibid.,* p. 59.
7. *Ibid.*
8. *Ibid.* p.65.
9. *Ibid.,* p. 66.
10. *Ibid.,* Pp.780-1.
11. *Chāndogya Upaniṣad,* 6.1.
12. Sri Aurobindo, *The Life Divine,* p. 284.
13. *Ibid.,* p. 302.
14. *Ibid.,* p. 298.
15. *Taittirīya Upaniṣad, Brahmānanda Valli,* 7.
16. Sri Aurobindo, *The Life Divine,* BK.1, p. 4.
17. *Ibid.,* vol.18, p. 40.
18. *Ibid.,* vol.1. p. 65.
19. *Ibid.,* p. 67.
20. *Ibid.,* vo.2, p. 853.
21. *Ibid.,* p. 661.
22. *Ibid.*
23. *Ibid.,* p. 839.
24. *Ibid.,* p. 704.
25. It is a view according to which the art-facts of science are given more importance than human values and life.
26. The excessive importance given to the ideas of any sort, which cannot be translated into concrete realities leads to the reification of those ideals. Such a position leads to empty transcendentalism.
27. *The Bhagavadgītā,* 16, 1-3.
28. In fact, the manifest forms of religious worship and participation in religious activities must be disassociated from spirituality.
29. Sri Aurobindo, *The Synthesis of Yoga,* Pondicherry: Sri Aurbindo Ashram, 1992, p. 929.
30. In a way the distinction between what is desired and what is desirable down to the distinction between 'is' and 'ought'. In other words, what is desired by an individual is a fact (is) and what is desirable for the society is (ought).
31. Sri Aurobindo, *Thoughts and Aphorisms*, Pondicherry: Sri Aurobindo Ashram, 1959, p. 55.
32. The purposive evolution of Sri Aurobindo explains the various stages of development of mind from the gross matter to the level of supramental consciousness. Thus the ascent of consciousness starts from its rudimentary stages to the highest level.

33. Sri Aurobindo. *The Life Divine.* Book 1, Pondicherry: Sri Aurobindo Ashram, 1990, p. 927.
34. The expression 'divine' in Sri Aurobindo's philosophy stands for purity.
35. Sri Aurobindo, *The Synthesis of Yoga,* p. 175.
36. Sri Aurobindo, *The Ideal of Humanity*. Pondicherry: Sri Aurobindo Ashram, 1971, Vol. 15, p. 278.
37. Sri Aurobindo, *The Human Cycle*. Pondicherry: Sri Aurobindo Ashram, 1950, P.278.
38. *Ibid.*
39. *Ibid.,* p. 279.
40. *Ibid.,* p. 56.

12

The Need for Comparative Philosophy

Introduction

Comparative philosophy is one of the most sought after disciplines in the contemporary times. We no more live in islands. Exchange of ideas for mutual benefit is the need of the hour. It is through the discipline called comparative philosophy such an exchange of ideas is possible. The traditions of the orient are relatively neglected by the scholars of oxidant for they believed that there is nothing worth the name philosophy in its proper sense. But this is not true as many scholars from the west explored the philosophical wisdom of the orient and they found the philosophical doctrines concerning metaphysics, epistemology, logic, ethics, aesthetics, philology, psychology and religion are highly insightful. The debates among the various philosophical schools within the Indian sub-continent are a lasting testimony to this fact.

In the oriental traditions, especially in the classical Indian tradition, the problems of philosophy invariably reflect the problems of life faced by the individuals in their day-to-day life. The solutions to these problems are found in the philosophical doctrines advanced by the various schools of thought in their own right. The source of the problem and how to put an end to a problem are discussed threadbare by the classical Indian philosophers. Therefore the philosophical doctrines advanced by the classical Indian philosophers are not merely meant for intellectual exercise, but are the solutions that are prescriptive in nature. It is the primacy of social welfare than anything else that dominated the spirit of the classical Indian tradition in which the incidental sciences have their own role to play. Philology, logic, soteriology, eschatology are also important for the enhancement of the quality of life. Although liberation is the ultimate goal of every individual, the social obligations of the individuals as moral agents are not to be ignored. Man and society are two sides of the same coin. One cannot exist without the other. Another important aspect to realize is that the essential human nature is same everywhere. Human welfare is a global priority.

Every culture has its own uniqueness and no culture is inferior to the other. We are living in societies that are by and large cosmopolitan in their nature. We need to move away from stereotypic way of thinking to invite new ways of thinking, new models of morality, and new forms of administration in order to make our philosophical tradition more pragmatic and meaningful. The elasticity of Indian mind shows that it welcomed new dimensions of philosophical activity by accepting the philosophical doctrines of the philosophers of Indian renaissance. Not only are we satisfied with a metaphysical principle which enables us to arrive at a particular conception of the world, we also look for the contribution of incidental sciences that are essential for any social activity. The classical Indian philosophical tradition did not ignore the role of individual in society. It has reminded every one of us to fulfill our obligations as moral agents insofar as our existence in the society is concerned. Thus it is highly pragmatic and taught us a way of life. *Dharmaśāstras* highlighted the significance of moral life both at individual and social levels. We just cannot set them aside because "since life is a whole, a unity, and its various phases cannot be left in isolation."[1]Society needs a good moral grounding for its social progress in general. Although one may not find an exclusive and systematic account of ethical doctrines, unlike in the west, classical Indian philosophers addressed the problems of morality in their own right. A comparative philosopher should not remain as a mere analyst, but he needs to synthesize the past, present and future. The new patterns of thought and action are possible only when we take into consideration the past. What the Indian philosophers have to imbibe from the west is the spirit of organization among other things. The guiding principle is already there in our philosophy as a metaphysical one. But it has to be related to our social life to make our empirical existence an authentic one. Therefore, we need to compare our philosophy with the rest of the philosophies advocated by the various philosophical traditions of the orient as well as oxidant for better understanding of human life.

Comparative Philosophy and It's Need

Hitherto what is called comparative philosophy is not all that sought after discipline, although some sort of comparisons we do make between certain concepts employed by one philosopher with those of the other. But this is done at the superficial level. The comparative attitude never penetrated into the core of the Indian mind. Also, it may be another reason that comparative philosophy did not really take off for we Indians underestimated our own philosophical tradition as inferior to the western philosophical tradition. This unfortunate imagination put down our own philosophical wisdom as something found wanting in many respects forgetting the fact that no philosophy is foolproof. The well acclaimed scholars of the west acknowledged that Indian has reached its spiritual heights. Therefore, there is no reason why we must be apologetic to the west in terms of our cultural heritage.[2]

The common objection against comparative philosophy is that it may dilute and misinterpret the cardinal doctrines of the various philosophical traditions of the east and the west. Late Professor Barlingay compared the Spinoza's conception of substance with that of Śaṅkara's Brahman. But one can notice the fundamental differences between their approaches. In many respects one can draw parallels between Spinoza's substance and Śaṅkara's Brahman. Both transcend the realm of discursive thought. Spinoza's pantheism clearly establishes the view that the world of objects is derived from the substance which is beyond discursive thought. As a mathematician Spinoza gives prominence to the method of deduction in his philosophy. For Śaṅkara deduction is not a legitimate method. He employs dialectical method which rests on the principle of non-contradiction.[3] In fact, the method of Śaṅkara can be compared with the method advocated by Bradley and Bosanquet. Sometimes even this comparison does not go well for Śaṅkara's method has negative implications, while the method of Bradley and Bosanquet has positive implications. But we come to know this fact only when we attempt to take a comparative approach. Although we say "comparison should be between system and system, but not between concept and concept."[4] As such this exercise may appear to be a bit difficult in the beginning, yet it is fruitful when we arrive at significant conclusions that will enable us to think afresh for better philosophical formulations. Such an enterprise helps us in recognizing the rationality present in the other philosophical traditions. Further we also come to know what is living and what is dead in any philosophical tradition. Our various patterns of life are somehow guided by scientific temper. But it has its own negative impact on the young minds because it infuses a kind of distrust of our *dharma,* our scriptural wisdom, and our philosophy in general. As a matter of fact, western scholars like Max Műeller have reposed faith in our *Dharmaśāstras,* our scriptural texts, and our philosophical tradition through comparative philosophy.

Another important factor is individuality that helps us in assessing the significance of any philosophical system. It is a living force by itself. We should not get carried away by the views of others. It is individuality which makes our decision making process to retain the vital elements of our past and to assimilate the new ideas that come from outside. This is possible only when we understand our own individuality. We have to compare our individuality with that of the others.[5] When we do comparative philosophy we come across new synthesis of ideas by comparing one system with the other. Comparison reveals valuable principles or ignored shortcomings. Either way we come to know something that is beneficial. There are also attempts by scholars to compare the doctrine of atomism of Vaiśeşika with that of Democritus of the ancient Greece. What is proved by modern science as regards atoms may not be present in them. But the very attempt to compare their views throws new light on the philosophical understanding of atomism. Similarly, the contribution made by the Jains, the Buddhists, and the philosophers of Nyāya-Vaiśeşika to logic may be compared with the Aristotelian logic.

Ultimately comparative philosophy leads us to a global philosophy. To quote Masson-Oursel, a French comparative philosopher, in this context, "the scope of comparative philosophy is as wide as the Universe."[6] Therefore, comparative philosophy as an important branch of philosophy must be encouraged for the better understanding of the traditions of the east and the west. After explaining the need for comparative philosophy, it appears paradoxical when we say that there is no philosophy called comparative philosophy just as saying that there is no religion called comparative religion. What we call comparative philosophy is nothing but the comparative study of philosophy. Hence "technically we have to fix the meaning of the term as the comparative study of eastern & western philosophies."[7] The chief motto of comparative philosophy is to renew the systematization of our thinking that includes all the given facts. At the same time it also transcends these very facts by adding something new to these facts in terms of interpretation.

Human Being as a Focal Point

What is man's place in comparative philosophy? This is an interesting question that dominates the very domain of comparative philosophy. Now the present era is not more the era of science, but it is the era of humanism. Now one can see in the contemporary philosophical scenario a shift in the attention of philosophers from self, God, matter, and science to human being. Thus, philosophy completely becomes anthropocentric. Even the analysts like Russell who criticized the culture and the philosophies of the Middle Ages, are of the opinion that it is of paramount importance of philosophy to preserve the values of human life. We certainly welcome new branches of philosophy, but not at the cost of basic human values. Human beings become the centre of attraction for all sorts of philosophizing under the title 'comparative philosophy'. All of us belong to the same species called 'humanity' in spite of our different outlooks and traditions. A comparative study of various philosophical traditions may provide us with some clues concerning the nature of human values which are of paramount importance to the entire human race. With this end in view, I propose to take up the following areas of comparative philosophy for further discussion. They are-1. The subject-matter of comparative philosophy, 2. Comparative philosophy and philosophical synthesis, and 3. The methods of comparative philosophy.

Comparative Philosophy and Its Subject-matter

This appears to be a difficult task for any student of comparative philosophy to deal with. But it appears that the subject-matter of comparative philosophy brings human being as an integral prat of any philosophical discussion of east or west. Our philosophy of action is rooted in human being as a moral agent. In the absence of human being it is as good as not doing any philosophy for all aspects of thought and action are attributed to human being alone. However, there are some aspects of thought and action that might have gained more prominence in the west than in the east. It simplifies our understanding of outlook of western man from that of eastern man. It also indicates that their views are one-sided. This does not mean that the essential nature of human being understood in the east is different from that portrayed in the west. The essential nature of human being is same everywhere. Every philosophical tradition tries to explain the nature of human being and his place in the universe. Human being as a historical being expresses himself in a variety of ways in different races and cultures. Comparative philosophy must study all these expressions of human being. Thus its scope becomes very wide.

Further, it is often asked: what is that we are going to compare with the real view to know the real nature of human being? Do we compare different cultures and histories of the various nations? Such an attempt has been made by comparing the history of Chinese with that of the Indians. Of course, the conclusions arrived at by comparing the histories of the various nations are certainly useful as we may come across the similarities and dissimilarities of the cultures of various nations. But the comparative study of cultures cannot be labelled as comparative philosophy. The subject-matter of comparative philosophy is the comparative study of the various philosophical traditions. Two different traditions may give importance to the same or similar values. Since these values are common to both the traditions, they may be interested in a particular form or aspect of life. At times different philosophical traditions uphold different values. For instance, the Chinese philosophers attached more importance to the values of human being and society in the world. They always aimed at knowing what kind of human value or life is the best to be sought after. But Indian philosophers, by and large, are interested in the reality of inwardness as against the outwarness of the reality. This is the case with almost every system in India, whether it is monistic or pluralistic, realistic or idealistic, activistic or quietistic.[8] As a matter of fact, every philosophical system developed certain aspects of human life to the highest level possible. In the process, it might have missed or ignored certain other aspects of human life. Comparative philosophy helps in tracing out what is missing in each philosophical tradition. In addition to that, we can also get clues to the solutions to various problems of life as advocated in each tradition. It is normally the case that different traditions uphold different values of life at different times. For example, it is very difficult to say whether western tradition is constantly outward or inward in its approach. Similar is the case with the Chinese tradition. The early classical schools of China had their own set of values of life, which are different from those of Buddhism. But over a period of time Buddhism got assimilated into the Chinese tradition. Therefore, it is only by means of comparative study of the various traditions one can know the values of life upheld by different traditions of philosophy at different times. The bottom line is that all the traditions inquire into the nature of human life from different perspectives.

There is another important aspect to be noticed. While doing comparative philosophy the strategies and the tools of inquiry may differ from tradition to tradition. It is the responsibility of the comparative philosopher to highlight the similarities and dissimilarities found in different traditions as regards the methods and results, and also their relevance to human life. To quote Radhakrishnan in this context:[9]

> The fundamentals human experience, which are the data of philosophical reflection, are the same everywhere. The transitoriness of all things, the play of chance, the emotions of love and hate, ear and jealousy, the continual presence of death, the anxiety to overcome the corruptibility of things, the fleeting moment--- and these have determined for each man his life's meaning and value.

Since the essential nature of all human beings one and same everywhere, understanding of human life and the world must be the sole concern of comparative philosophy. If it lacks such an orientation, then the alternative would be to find out whether a given system is idealistic, realistic, naturalistic, monistic, materialist, organsistic, etc. For this purpose one need not approach comparative philosophy. Classification of various philosophical systems is one thing, and the evaluation of comparative philosophy is another.

When we consider human being as the centre of our study, we do not intend to study only one aspect of human being rather human activity as a whole. Human being can be studied from the points of view of materialism, teleology, psychology, sociology, ethics, religion, and so on. This because human being is a complex creature "leading an inward and outward life and craving stable support both ways."[10] But each approach listed above in itself is inadequate to unravel the complete nature of human being. The more we dwell upon human being, the more we come to know about him. The complete nature of human being is the ideal set forth before comparative philosophy. This is what is called human being's philosophy of life.

The question that is asked frequently is: Is the essential nature of all human beings same? If it is so, why is that the man of orient is differentiated from the man of occident as if they belong to two different species? The oriental man is often characterized as intuitive, lethargic, spiritual, mystical, introvert, and contended; while the occidental man is characterized as rational, active, materialistic, ethical, extrovert, and discounted. This differentiation is highly subjective and is not accepted by all. Radhakrishnan maintains that human being is basically the same though there are differences in the various cultures in which he is brought up. Human beings share same urges, instincts, aspirations, and ideals. When we compare the oriental man with the occidental man, are we trying to compare their cultural achievements or innate capabilities? A psychologist's comparison of two different individuals is always in terms of their intelligent quotient (IQ), but not in terms of their cultural achievements. Likewise, when we want to understand the essential nature of human being we should not compare them on the basis of their cultural achievements, but we should look into their essential nature that is common to all human beings. Without such an orientation comparative philosophy becomes unproductive. In order to substantiate our view we can argue that when a psychologist studies human being in terms of emotion, sensations, thought, etc., the general laws that he/she formulates about human beings are universally applicable to all of them. If it is not so, then his findings of the western psychologists are of little use to the psychologists of the east and vice-versa. Because of this reason one has to assume *a priori* that the fundamental nature of all human beings is the same.

This is the first principle of comparative philosophy. Human being is a creative creature. He is capable of creating culture, framing ideals, and transforming them. But human being's creativity does not exhaust his essential nature. He is capable of adapting himself to the changing environment, social or natural. What is after all to be noticed here is that human being behind the culture is more important than the cultures, which may progress or decay.

There is no philosophy or ideology that claims to have no respect for human life and the will-to-live although ideologies and philosophies can vary from one nation to the other. If the fulfilment of human life and human values is the aim of every ideology or philosophy, then it is the meeting point for all of them. Human being's knowledge of life was vague and indefinite in the beginning due to lack of adequate theory of knowledge. Hence any attempt to derive human being's philosophy of life from his theory of knowledge would result in an incomplete picture of his life. The best way to understand human being's philosophy of life is to make his theory of knowledge subservient to his life. By doing so his life will not be at risk even if his theory of knowledge is not perfect. The dictum 'knowledge for the sake of knowledge' can be entertained when knowledge is unbiased. Only such unbiased knowledge alone can discover truth, which is a true human value. But knowledge as power helps human beings in controlling and dominating brutal natural forces that are disastrous for the furtherance of human race. To this extent Francis Bacon is right in saying that 'knowledge is power'. The discoveries and inventions of human beings in the various fields of investigation must be conducive to human life, and not detrimental to it. A world-view becomes a true guide to human life when it promotes values conducive to human life. Therefore, the task of comparative philosophy is to revive original integral outlook in a better articulated form so that a proper world-philosophy can be developed. In other words, the genuine aim of comparative philosophy is to create and promote metaphysical humanism, which is nothing but a world-view of human life and for human life.

Is Philosophical Synthesis Possible?

Well, a genuine comparative philosopher's answer to this question is always positive. In fact, the process of interaction and mutual understanding between the orient and occident is in progress. The separation of the orient from the occident on flimsy grounds is no more acceptable. The traditions of the orient and the occident contributed to the furtherance of human race on the globe in their own right. In some parts of the globe we could witness rapid changes and in some parts of the globe we do not. This does not mean human beings are different in different places. The progress of any culture depends upon various geographical as well as social factors. The wants and needs of people are different due to their geographical locations. Partly, their cultures are influenced by these geographical factors. But these artificial division of the orient and the occident disappears once we realize the highest universal ideals that are common to all human beings. The true human values that are hitherto unknown to many cultures, will be brought to their notice. These universal values would be received by all cultures alike. Thus "the problems and solutions to of one culture will be the problems and solutions for all."[11] However, some cultures may face problems initially to accommodate these universal human values. Gradually they realize the importance of these values, and pave the way for their assimilation into their cultures. Only comparative philosophers can help the people to understand the significance of these universal values for a broader and deep perspective of human life. Such perspective alone can be characterized as 'world perspective', which can lead to global philosophy. Unlike other systems of philosophy, global philosophy is not a system of philosophy belonging to a set of individuals, but it belongs to the entire humankind. Its sole objective would be to maintain harmonious intercultural relations.

The Methods of Comparative Philosophy

Humanism as a philosophy could not receive much respect from the academics, for they feared that it is opposed to metaphysics and logic. But it is not the case. The philosophers of the past have advanced world-views keeping their race, nation or community in their mind. Not only that, they have maintained that whatever is advocated by them is applicable to entire human race. But the fact remains that each of them have produced world-philosophies that have limited application to human race. On the contrary, a comparative philosopher must transcend these limitations to evolve a world-philosophy for a better cohesion of humanity. Both the harmony of life and the cohesion of humanity would be the chief concern of a comparative philosopher. Now we have to look for a right method to achieve such an ideal. We have to understand human being's inner being. How do we know? This is an important question to be tackled by a comparative philosopher.

The correct approach to comparative philosophy must be from philosophy, and the methods to be employed must also be the methods of philosophy. What are such methods? In what way the methods of philosophy are different from those of psychology, ethnology, philology, anthropology, sociology, etc.? The methods of philosophy are reflection and evaluation. A comparative philosophers reflects over and evaluates critically the various values recognized by different philosophical traditions. Thus comparative philosophy is more concerned with values than with the facts presented by the various sciences. This is how it differs from the other sciences, although it does not oppose the facts presented by other sciences. No science can supply criteria for philosophy. By presenting the facts of life, these disciplines simply tell us what the case is. But they cannot provide us with any solution. The task of finding a right solution is left to the philosopher.

The philosophers like Paul Masson-Oursel, Kwee Swan Liat, and F.S.C. Northrop approached comparative philosophy from a phenomenological point of view. Each of them tried to show the circumstances under which a philosopher had developed his philosophy. In other words, they tried to show the relation of the philosopher to his social environment. However, this is not to deny their contribution made to comparative philosophy. In other words, they tried to show the relation of a philosophers to his social environment. Their works definitely remain significant and important as descriptive and positivistic studies. The very activity of philosophizing is to gain an insight into the nature of human being and the world with a view to elucidate the meaning and purpose of human life. Phenomenology as a method cannot serve this purpose. However, Liat realized the shortcomings of the phenomenological method and suggested a kind of meta-philosophy to evaluate the values advanced by the various philosophical traditions. Now the question arises: what should be criterion of evaluation? The essential human values that transcend all limitations must be our criteria. How do we arrive at such human values? It is through reflection on our own experiences. The term 'experience' should not be taken in its narrower sense; rather it should be understood in terms of inward and outward expressions of human being. Hence self-reflection must be starting point of our study. In order to keep an open mind, a philosopher must be honest and sincere in his attempts to inquire into the truth. He must be as self-critical as he is towards others. He must be a model to others.

Of course, the standards of evaluation are not readymade like logical calculus. A comparative philosopher has to evolve the criteria from his own life experiences. May be the experiences of human beings differ from one individual to the other. But these differences can be taken care of by comparison and evaluation. The differences are due to some hidden inclinations that an individual has towards certain things of the world. Another important factor is mutual tolerance. It is absolutely necessary to be tolerant to others' views. Unanimity in opinions can be arrived at by artificial means too. But they are highly unphilosophical and unprogressive. Such cooked up opinions should not be entertained.

Concluding Remarks

Although comparative philosophy is a fruitful exercise, there are many who think that it is impossible to undertake as it involves ideals like tolerance and open-mindedness. The general perception is that the philosophical traditions in the orient in general are spiritual, practical and other-worldly, and the philosophical traditions in the west are intellectual and this worldly. How can there be any comparison between two diametrically opposite traditions? For instance, if one says that comparison between Indian and western philosophical traditions is not possible is to say that we refuse to understand each other. Today we have transcended the limits of dialogue and entered into the realm of polylogue. There are many western scholars who understood Indian philosophy and also wrote extensively on various themes of Indian philosophy. Similarly, there are many Indian scholars who understood the philosophical doctrines of the west and wrote extensively on them. Mutual understanding is the first step towards comparative philosophy. The conceptual or thought schema of the western philosophers are understood through their own conceptual schema of Indian philosophers. Such a welcoming of ideas from others' tradition would enhance the mutual understanding and interpretation of concepts. Therefore, the Kiplingian dictum "East is East and the West is West, and never the twain shall meet"[12] does not hold water anymore.

There is one more objection against comparative philosophy. How can we compare Indian philosophy, which is popularly known as *darśana*, with western philosophy, which is nothing but 'love of wisdom'? It has become a fashion to call Indian philosophy practical, and western philosophy theoretical. This is a misconception. The philosophies of Plato, Aristotle, and Hegel are practice-oriented as they intended to develop the doctrines of political, ethical, and social action. We cannot simply brand a philosophical tradition as theoretical or practical, activistic or quietistic without understanding the context in which these terms are used in different realms of man's being. If we fail to notice this fact, the result is 'the fallacy of misplaced comparisons'.[13] Although the word '*darśana*' means 'seeing', it should be understood as 'viewing'. Different *darśanas* of classical Indian tradition have presented different views about the truth. Truth is one but the views about truth are many. Similarly, the statement that philosophy is 'love of wisdom' is also misinterpreted. Greek philosophers were not merely interested in transmitting us the 'love of wisdom'; they have also bequeathed to us well defined philosophical doctrines. So is the case with Indian philosophers. Hence, to say that Indian and Western philosophies cannot be compared because the former is *darśana* and the latter is philosophy is to commit what is one may call 'the fallacy of etymological misapplication'.[14]

In spite of all these speed breakers, one can still pursue comparative philosophy for otherwise we miss the other's perspective. The synthesis of the various ideals projected by different philosophical traditions of the orient and the occident enhances the scope of philosophy. Philosophy does not belong to no man's land. It is philosophy of life, for it brings together facts (is) and values (ought). This kind of synthesis of ideals should not be treated as eclecticism Thus comparative philosophy being human-centred would lead to a new kind of humanism.

Notes

1. P.T.Raju, *Thought and Reality, Hegelianism and Advaita,* London: Allen & Unwin, 1937, p. 20.
2. *Ibid.,* p. 24.
3. P.T. Raju, "The Outcry against Comparative Philosophy, " *Aryan Path,* Vol.6, 1935, p. 98.
4. *Ibid.*
5. P.T. Raju, *Thought and Reality, Hegelianism and Advaita,* p. 27.
6. P.T. Raju, *Introduction to Comparative Philosophy*, Nebraska: University of Nebraska Press, 1962, p. 283.
7. P.T. Raju, *Lectures on Comparative Philosophy,* Poona: University of Poona Press, 1970, p. 2.
8. P.T. Raju, *Introduction to Comparative Philosophy*, p. 285.
9. *Ibid.,* p. 2. (Introduction by S.Radhakrishnan)
10. See P.T. Raju's 'Introduction' in S. Radhakrishnan and P.T. Raju (eds.) *The Concept of Man: A Study in Comparative Philosophy,* Nebraska: University of Nebraska Press, 1960, p. 24.
11. P.T. Raju, *Introduction to Comparative Philosophy*, p. 288.
12. *Ibid.*
13. P.T.Raju, *Lectures on Comparative Philosophy*, p. 66.
14. *Ibid.,* p. 67.

Index